Table of Contents

Preface

During the 1990s, the international aid community has directed much of its attention to dealing with civil wars and their aftermath. In the wake of somewhat disjointed efforts to promote peace and reconstruction, there has been an attempt to structure a more integrated approach towards peace-making, rehabilitation and development. Dealing with problems of psychological distress and the disruption of local systems of social support and solidarity has been a particularly difficult aspect of this task. Such problems have a crucial bearing on people's ability to rebuild their lives and society's social fabric.

Children of War: Responses to Psycho-Social Distress in Cambodia, by Jo Boyden and Sara Gibbs, examines the relationship between conflict and psycho-social distress; how children, their families and communities are affected by war and social upheaval; and the appropriateness of national and international responses to psycho-social problems.

The authors reveal the complex nature of psycho-social distress and the ways in which its effects are mediated by a range of conditions related, for example, to socio-economic conditions, cultural contexts and values, access to services, family circumstances and an individual's characteristics. From this analysis emerges a critique of the role of international and national agencies. While many agencies recognize that this is an important area for intervention, some are at a loss as to how to intervene; others have often applied therapeutic models that are inappropriate both in terms of their cost and human resource requirements, as well as in their basic assumptions about the nature and effects of trauma and who constitutes a vulnerable group.

Children of War provides useful guidance to agencies and individuals working in this field. The challenge to aid and social service agencies is how to find an appropriate balance between indigenous strategies and external interventions; and how to support certain local in-stitutions and coping strategies. As the authors point out, this implies that external agencies must embark on a comprehensive learning process about the role of indigenous systems of healing; how Cam-bodians themselves perceive and understand suffering, illness and vulnerability; and their coping strategies.

The findings stress the importance of confronting psychological problems at the community level, and borrowing from approaches in the field of physical health in which low-cost preventive measures take precedence over secondary care involving expensive imported drugs and trained medical staff. The authors recommend that the aid community should look to ways of supporting certain community institutions that provide social and cultural support and the training of community-based para-professionals.

Two initiatives came together to make this study possible. In 1994, the United Nations Research Institute for Social Development (UNRISD) launched a research programme on **Vulnerability and Coping Strategies in Cambodia**. This programme examined various aspects of the rebuilding process, one of which involved issues of psycho-social vulnerability. The International Develop-ment Research Centre (IDRC) in Canada and the United Nations

Children's Fund (UNICEF) actively supported work on these issues and organized, in early 1995, a consultative process in Cambodia to understand better how Cambodians themselves view psycho-social problems. This inquiry revealed considerable ambiguity and uncertainty in the way different cultures, social groups and institutions perceive and respond to psycho-social distress. As a precursor to a longer-term study on these issues, IDRC, UNICEF and UNRISD decided to engage the authors of this monograph to set out systematically the key concepts, indicators and issues related to psycho-social vulnerability, and to provide a preliminary assessment of the role of national and international agencies in this field.

The second initiative evolved out of United Nations General Assembly resolution 48/157 passed in 1993, which called for a comprehensive research programme to study the complex and multi-dimensional problems facing children affected by situations of armed conflict. The resulting **United Nations Study on the Impact of Armed Conflict on Children**, headed by Graça Machel, undertook a series of regional consultations and case studies. Within the framework of this inquiry, the "Machel study" supported the present work on psycho-social distress in Cambodia.

UNRISD would like to thank the following people and their institutions for facilitating this project: Anne Bernard and Andrew McNaughton (IDRC), Margaret de Monchy (UNICEF-Cambodia), Cathie Guthrie (UNICEF-Canada), Stuart Maslen (UN Study on the Impact of Armed Conflict on Children) and Brian Pratt (International NGO Training and Research Centre-INTRAC).

UNRISD work on **Vulnerability and Coping Strategies in Cambodia** is co-ordinated by Peter Utting and is supported by a grant from DANIDA.

Dharam Ghai
Director, UNRISD

Acknowledgements

During the course of both the research and the writing of this report many people gave us valuable advice and assistance. In Cambodia special thanks are due to: Margie de Monchy at UNICEF and Valerie Taton and Denis Bribosia at the UNHCR for all their encouragement and generous hospitality; to IDRC for hosting the roundtable meetings of the "Working Group on Psycho-Social Vulnerability and Coping Strategies in Cambodia", and also to all its members who shared with us their thoughts and feelings. Somphal Paidra provided invaluable research assistance, as did Thoin Sean Lay at Krom Akphiwat Phum. The vast majority of the people with whom we spoke are not, however, mentioned by name here; we would nevertheless like to thank them all for giving so generously of their time in order to share with us their insights and reflections on the situation in Cambodia.

Stuart Maslen and Peter Utting provided continuous guidance and support; their detailed comments on earlier drafts, alongside those from David Drucker, Peter Loizos, Man Hau Liev, Paula Uimonen and members of the working group in Cambodia were extremely valuable and where possible have been incorporated. We are also greatly indebted to Thanak for his translation of Khmer scripts and to Cleo Small of INTRAC for her editorial work. Thanks also goes to Lauren Engle from UNRISD for editorial assistance and design,

Anita Tombez for secretarial assistance, and Jenifer Freedman for editorial advice and overall management. Responsibility for the content of this final draft, however, naturally remains with the authors.

Dr. Jo Boyden is an anthropologist and senior social development consultant. She has worked internationally with non-governmental, intergovernmental and governmental organizations, particularly with respect to especially disadvantaged children, including children affected by armed conflict. Co-author of **Families** with UNESCO and **Children of the Cities** with Pat Holden she has also produced several major UNICEF reports on children's work.

Sara Gibbs currently heads the INTRAC NGO Sector Analysis Programme that provides NGOs with an on-going analysis of key strategic trends in the context of a rapidly changing NGO environment. Sara studied medical anthropology at Brunel University. She has conducted ethnographic research on the affects of conflict on children in Mozambique for Save The Children Fund/UK and co-authored an annotated bibliography for Radda Barnen on research methods with children affected by organized violence.

Foreword

This report is based on field research in Cambodia conducted by the authors over a period of seven weeks towards the end of 1995. It draws on both primary and secondary Cambodian sources, as well as a theoretical and practical understanding of childhood issues in other countries in conflict and transition.

We were assigned the task of assessing perceptions and factors of resilience and vulnerability among children, their families and communities in Cambodia in the context of two and a half decades of political violence and social upheaval, as well as examining the nature of national and international institutional responses. Our investigation was to focus particularly on psycho-social issues, this word being used advisedly in place of the now widely employed term "trauma", which invokes a fairly narrow and prescriptive Western, biomedical framework. Psycho-social distress, on the other hand, we understand as referring broadly to a variety of difficulties affecting individuals, from mental health disorders, behavioural problems and somatic symptoms, to distortions in moral learning. We suggest, moreover, that psycho-social distress is less an expression of individual pathological response to catastrophe and more a reflection of the subjective ways in which individuals engage with their environment in the context of political violence and other stressful events.

Given the time allowed for the work, and the fact that we were able to visit only one province outside Phnom Penh, the findings are necessarily partial. Indeed, we do not attempt to come up with a comprehensive "Cambodian" or "expatriate" perspective, the aim being rather to identify key issues, raise important questions and suggest possible areas for further research and action. In relation to the assignment we were given, the major weakness of the study in our view is the serious shortage of information about Cambodian children specifically. This is partly because there is very little information and knowledge about the psycho-social condition of children in Cambodia and partly because there was insufficient time for doing much primary research directly with children during our fieldwork.

We used a variety of methods for gathering the data. These included: a review of published and unpublished materials on Cambodia; roundtable and focus group discussions; key informant interviews; semi-structured interviews; time lines, life histories and observation. Respondents in Phnom Penh included staff in multilateral, bilateral, governmental and non-governmental agencies (national and international) and academic and religious organizations. Fieldwork in Battambang province was conducted both in the town of Battambang itself and in one village in particular, although several other villages were also visited briefly. It involved interviews and observation with both children and adults: residents, returnees and displaced people, Phum (village) leaders and traditional healers, monks, nuns, shop-keepers, development workers and teachers. Our research with children was conducted in the places where they were working and playing and drawings were used to focus and prompt discussion.

We were surprised by the large amount of secondary material on conflict in Cambodia and the interest in many quarters in psycho-social issues. In aid circles particularly, there is a lively debate about the psycho-social impacts of political violence and the appropriate institutional responses. This debate is fed by a wide range of perspectives and views: reflecting the theoretical inadequacy of the social sciences in the face of political violence and other extreme forms of human behaviour. On this, David Drucker comments:

Perhaps even more than in physics the social sciences have nowhere yet the remotest outline of a unified theory of human behaviour which embraces the bio-physical, psychological, individual, family, group, community, national, international, social, economic, political, religious, and spiritual. Therefore, by necessity, we resort to fragmentary examination of the human condition and find it difficult, if not impossible, to give appropriate weight to one set of findings in relation to another (personal communication).

Gary Ladd and Ed Cairns also take up the argument, lamenting the absence of an "enduring community" of researchers devoted to understanding the effects of political and ethnic violence on children in particular: "research on ethnic and political violence does not have an identity within contemporary scientific communities . . . nor does its mission fit well into national and international research priorities and funding 'categories'" (1996:16). Then there is the problem, again highlighted by Drucker, that most of the academic disciplines that are prominent internationally are "in fact profoundly culturally determined by their origins in **Western** observation, experience and thinking. . . ." He continues by commenting that: "It is only recently that this Western orientation has been shown to have obscured much of what is significant in non-Western societies in general, and, in Cambodia in particular, this has led to much confusion in understanding and proved to be dysfunctional in practice" (personal communication). This report does not attempt to resolve these confusions so much as point to some of the inconsistencies and gaps in the way people — Cambodians and expatriates — frame and respond to psycho-social issues in Cambodia.

Acronyms

AIDS	Acquired Immune Deficiency Syndrome
CFDS	Cambodia Family Development Services
CMAC	Cambodian Mine Action Centre
CMHTP	Cambodia Mental Health Training Programme
COFRAS	Compagnie française d'assistance spéciale
CWDA	Cambodian Women's Development Association
EU	European Union
HIV	Human Immunodeficiency Virus
HPTC	Harvard Programme in Refugee Trauma Cambodia
IDRC	International Development Research Centre
ILO	International Labour Organisation
IMF	International Monetary Fund
IMR	Infant Mortality Rate
INTRAC	The International NGO Training and Research Centre
IOM	International Organization for Migration
IPSER	Institute for Psycho-Social and Socio-Ecological Research
IRC	International Rescue Committee
KBS	Khmer Buddhist Society
Licadho	Cambodian League for the Promotion and Defense of Human Rights
MAG	Mines Advisory Group

MSALVA	Ministry of Social Affairs and Labour and Veterans' Association
NGO	non-governmental organization
ODA	Overseas Development Administration
OSB	Overseas Bureau of Australia
PADV	Project Against Domestic Violence
PERC	Programme de réhabilitation et appui au secteur agricole de Cambodge (Rehabilitation and Support Programme for the Agricultural Sector of Cambodia)
PKR	People's Republic of Kampuchea
PTSD	Post-Traumatic Stress Disorder
SNC	Supreme Nations Council
UN	United Nations
UNBRO	United Nations Border Relief Operations
UNDP	United Nations Development Programme
UNHCR	Office of the United Nations High Commissioner for Refugees
UNICEF	United Nations Children's Fund
UNRISD	United Nations Research Institute for Social Development
UNTAC	United Nations Transitional Authority in Cambodia
WB	World Bank

CAMBODIA

Extracted from: Utting P. 1994 *Between Hope and Insecurity:*
The Social Consequences of the Cambodian Peace Process, UNRISD,
Geneva, Switzerland.

PART 1

International Perspectives on Psycho-Social Distress in Children

This Cambodian boy is returning with his family to Svay Chek, a provincial city from which many people fled because of renewed fighting and landmine explosions. Credit: UNICEF/5705/Mainichi/Shinichi Asabe.

1.1

Introduction

Today Cambodians both remember and forget. The pains they suffered, as individuals, as members of crushed families, are deeply ingrained and the wounds will probably never heal. But the catastrophe seems to remain circumscribed in personal history. Paradoxically, this period of totally collective life developed into an individualistic struggle for life, aimed at surviving and, later, at re-establishing some normalcy (Thion, 1993:181).

The impact of political violence and the disruption it causes to people's lives is currently a major concern globally, not just for affected communities, but also among governments and national and

international non-governmental agencies. There has in recent decades been a significant increase in the number of conflicts reported.
Although the figures vary widely, Duffield (1994) notes a rise from
about 10 in 1960 to around 50 today. According to UNDP (1994)
the vast majority of these conflicts are internal: "only 3 of the 82
conflicts between 1989 and 1992 were between States" (Goodhand,
1994:14). Most of the recent conflicts have occurred in the developing world and those on the front-line have mainly been civilians, the
proportion of civilian casualties as opposed to military being over 90
per cent in some cases (Summerfield, 1991; Boyden, 1994).

The severity of the impact of conflict on civilians, both adults and
children, is not in doubt. But the form it takes and how individuals are
thought to respond, and how they can best be supported in coping, is
more controversial. Western ideologies have had a profound influence
on aid policy and intervention in many countries (Williams, 1996) and
inform the discourse as to who is most vulnerable and in what ways
they become vulnerable to stress. The Western view is that children
are especially and universally vulnerable to stress: generally seen as
passive recipients of experience rather than active negotiators of it. In
the context of conflict specifically, they are cast as victims. Yet the
evidence points to the unpredictability of children's responses to
political violence: the resourcefulness of many children in the face of
extreme adversity has led to a search for those factors which mediate
psycho-social impact. At one time the psychological literature focused
almost exclusively on personal factors such as age, sex and personality.
However, few studies ever examined these systematically and as a
result it is impossible to draw any clear conclusions as to their influence
on resilience and vulnerability (Cairns, 1996:168). More recent social
research has emphasized the contextual factors mediating impact,
such as the nature of the stressful event, the child's position in that
event, the integrity of social networks and economic resilience. In
practice the forces operating at the individual and structural levels are
intimately linked and interact closely. Accordingly, a full analysis of

the psycho-social well-being of children affected by political violence needs to be set within a broad framework which encompasses the personal and contextual factors mediating vulnerability and resilience.

One of the dominant paradigms shaping aid interventions in conflict zones is the Western psycho-therapeutic model based on the biomedical concept of trauma. However, the relevance and appropriateness of theoretical assumptions drawing on biomedical notions of health and illness and on Western definitions and understandings of childhood to societies that have very different ontologies and social and cultural forms, is increasingly being brought into question. People are now doubting both the validity of Western psychiatric models across cultures and the notion of childhood as a time of passivity, vulnerability and dependency.

The following section assesses these theoretical assumptions by discussing their origin, development and practical application. In Part 2 the study examines the factors mediating the impact of conflict at the individual, family and community level, Part 3 outlines the impact of the Cambodian conflict on adults and children. Finally, Part 4 examines contrasting perceptions of and responses to conflict among Khmer and expatriates living and working in Cambodia. The concluding section summarizes the study's main findings and suggests ways in which external agencies might play a more constructive role in addressing psycho-social issues in Cambodia.

1.2

The Thinking Behind
Psycho-Social Interventions

Identifying psycho-social impacts on children

At one time, international effort in the context of political violence was directed at satisfying "basic needs" such as health, nutrition, shelter and safety. However, awareness of the many adverse psycho-social impacts of conflict on civilian populations is now growing, as are the number of interventions in this field. Anxiety about the effects of war on children specifically has intensified over the course of the twentieth century, the initial impetus having been the work with refugee children in Europe following the First World War of Eglantyne Jebb, founder of The Save the Children Fund. Awareness of the full extent of possible implications for children has, however, become apparent only recently. No longer is concern limited to physical impacts such as wounding or death, or to problems such as family separation and displacement, since it is now apparent that many children are also affected by overt abuses such as sexual exploitation and violence, informal justice, forced labour, corruption and banditry.

It is most likely that children in early childhood and in the initial years of mid-childhood have specific susceptibilities to violence due to their immaturity and minority status in society. The collapse of traditional authority structures, decline of social networks, weakening of cultural and spiritual values and disruption of gender roles may undermine children's socialization, for example, leading to a loss of survival and social skills. Changes in the demographic structure of households and communities, together with family impoverishment, drastically reduce the age thresholds for marriage, child-bearing, work and decision-making, forcing children to assume social and economic responsibilities that lead to increases in exposure to physical danger and exploitation.

Young children often take their cue from their adult carers. Emotional or behavioural changes in adults, such as extreme protectiveness or authoritarianism, may be incomprehensible to them and cause serious anxiety. Seeing their parents or other important adults in their lives become vulnerable emotionally can severely undermine children's confidence. A decline in the capacity of families to provide positive reinforcement for children may be aggravated by the demise of peer groupings and loss of peer reference points, leaving them isolated socially.

Children exposed to political violence may experience a range of difficulties. These include behaviour problems, somatic complaints, mental health disorders and impaired moral reasoning and cognitive functioning. Although difficult to assess, some researchers have suggested that school absenteeism and juvenile crime (Cairns, 1987), or attitudes favouring gambling, pre-marital sexual intercourse and smoking (Greer, 1985) could indicate altered moral learning in children. However, some of these behaviours could also be interpreted as pragmatic strategies for survival in a situation of adversity. Other authors have measured physical aggression, imitation of military acts and unwillingness to co-operate with peers as indicators of developmental damage (see, for example, Leyens and Mahjoub, undated). And the tendency of young people to adopt uncompromising or extreme attitudes has also been explained by Greer as implying a delay in the development of moral reasoning.

Indications of severe mental distress in children resemble those experienced by adults. Symptoms include depression, feelings of helplessness, anxiety, fear, instability, agitation, low self-esteem, paranoia and confusion (Rutter, 1994; Richman, 1992). Extreme inflexibility and sad or suicidal feelings are also common acute reactions. Beginning some time after the stressful event, children may experience numbing of responsiveness to or reduced involvement with the external world. This may be indicated by a markedly diminished interest in activities and surroundings, feelings of detachment or estrangement from others, loss of energy, or withdrawal. Children who are deeply distressed may be affected by memory loss or lack of concentration and may be extremely restless. They may be very irritable or have recurrent and intrusive recollections of the stressful event.

Somatic symptoms such as poor appetite, eating too much, breathing difficulties, pains and dizziness are common in children exposed to political violence. Some children lose recently acquired skills and faculties, such as keeping dry at night. Nightmares and sleep disturbances and hyper-vigilance are widespread reactions, as is nervousness, irritability and fearfulness (Thomas, 1990 cited in Cairns, 1996:33). Children may have difficulties in their personal relationships with others: they may be too sad and withdrawn to want to play with other children, or unable to trust or show affection to adults for fear they may disappear. Some children experience deep feelings of guilt about surviving when others have not, or indeed about what they had to do in order to survive (Rutter, 1994; Richman, 1992). Some of those affected by political conflict remain psychologically vulnerable and a few may manifest chronic, often highly debilitating, disorders. Among the children who suffer severe reactions, the symptoms tend to become worse with time (Cairns, 1996:168).

Ascribing meaning to human distress

Research in different countries and conflicts suggests that children's psycho-social responses to violence have many universal features: ". . . because of the psychodynamic process being the same in humans, regardless of the culture and country of origin of the person" (Winkelmann, 1996:48). This does not, however, signify a consensus among social scientists on psycho-social issues: on the contrary, the topic is surrounded by controversy. The debate has been partly informed by research and therapeutic work conducted in Europe during and after the Second World War. Much of this early research focused on the impact of conflict on children. More recently, though, international thinking on psycho-social issues has been shaped by investigations conducted in the United States with veterans of the Viet Nam war. This led to the development and broad acceptance of a syndrome, Post-Traumatic Stress Disorder (PTSD), as being a specific manifestation of psycho-social distress associated with exposure to political violence and similar catastrophes. The identification of PTSD and its inclusion in the DSM-III psychiatric manual in the early 1980s gave social meaning to the suffering of veterans, as well as making it possible for them to claim benefits from the state through litigation.

PTSD is said to be precipitated by a distinct stressor that is generally outside the range of usual human experience and of sufficient intensity to invoke significant symptoms of distress from almost anyone. Existence of this stressor is the first diagnostic criterion for PTSD. Another criterion is the re-experiencing of the trauma, as evidenced by at least one of the following: recurrent and intrusive recollections of the event; recurrent dreams of the event; and sudden acting or feeling as if the traumatic event were reoccurring, because of an association with an environmental or ideational stimulus. A third criterion consists of the numbing of responsiveness to or reduced involvement with the external world, beginning some time after the trauma, as shown by at least one of the following: markedly diminished interest in one or more significant activities; feeling of detachment or estrangement from others; and constricted affect. A fourth category consists of at least two symptoms that were not present before the trauma, drawn from the following range: hyper alertness or exaggerated startle response; sleep disturbance; guilt about surviving when others have not, or about behaviour required for survival; memory impairment or trouble concentrating; avoidance of activities that arouse recollection of the traumatic event; and intensification of symptoms through exposure to events that symbolize or resemble the traumatic event. A broad distinction is made between chronic and acute reactions:

> An acute reaction represents a normal shock reaction which follows exposure to a highly stressful event. It generally lasts for only a few days and is marked by features of severe anxiety. Chronic reactions, on the other hand, are those which endure beyond this brief time span and include a persistence of often

debilitating symptoms. The chronic reaction in adults is marked by post-traumatic stress disorder, but in children takes a more diversified form including age-appropriate symptoms of stress (Gibson, 1989:660-661).

It is also posited that reactions can be grouped into phases — the impact phase, the recoil phase and the post-traumatic phase — each one of which is characterized by different needs and different modes of expression of distress.

PTSD is now thought by many internationally to describe the reactions of both civilians and the military to a wide variety of situations associated with conflict and other traumatic events. Although initially perceived to apply to adults, several researchers have begun to suggest that children may also display symptoms approximating PTSD. Thus, it is said that the exposure of children to one or more identifiable stressors (such as violence, separation from family, displacement from home) is expressed in symptoms which, when manifested together with two or more other such symptoms constitute PTSD (Gibbs, 1994:270).

That PTSD originated in the field of psychiatry in the United States is significant because it locates the syndrome firmly within the Western biomedical tradition. Biomedicine is based on very specific Western European cultural conceptions, heavily influenced by the seventeenth century French philosopher Descartes, and yet the model has now gained currency throughout the world. As with any belief system, biomedicine is based on an assumption that it objectively describes reality and that this reality is valid everywhere. However, even though it has widespread credence among health and welfare workers internationally, biomedicine is not the only authentic model for understanding and intervening in health and illness. Indeed, although biomedicine is based on rational scientific principles, it is "increasingly being understood as one of many medicines . . . culturally and historically distinct, specific and far from universal" (Gordon, 1988:20). The Chinese medical system, for example, which was developed some 2,000 years ago and remains one of the most important models in the world today, is founded in a very different philosophy and draws on very different principles.

To understand more fully some of the difficulties with making universal claims for the biomedical model, it is worth looking at how biomedicine conceives of the individual in ways that are very different from those in non-Western societies. In the biomedical tradition the origin of illness and disease is located within the physically bounded body — which is understood to function as the receptacle of the mind. Although the "mind" is located within the "body", they are nevertheless seen as separate and distinguishable entities; the cause of illness residing in one or the other. Other philosophical traditions, however, have very different views on this:

> . . . many ethno-medical systems do not logically distinguish body, mind and self, and therefore illness cannot be situated in body or mind alone. Social relations are also understood as key contributors to individual health and illness. In short, the body is seen as a unitary, integrated aspect of self and social relations. It is dependent on, and vulnerable to, the feelings, wishes, and actions of others, including spirits and dead ancestors. The body is not understood as a vast complex machine, but rather as a microcosm of the universe (Scheper-Hughes and Lock, 1989:21).

Some observers suggest also that by medicalizing people's problems and giving primacy to individual pathology, biomedicine depoliticizes human distress:

> . . . investing authority in biomedical reasoning about human problems eliminates explanations of disorders at levels of

psychological, political and economic functioning. Consequently, problems with origins in poverty, discrimination, role conflict and so forth are treated medically (Higginbotham and Marsella cited in Bracken et al., 1995:20).

The illness dimension of human distress is being medicalized and individualized rather than politicized and collectivized. Medicalization inevitably entails a missed identification between the individual and the social bodies and a tendency to transform the social into the biological (Lock and Scheper-Hughes, 1990:53).

It is vital to understand the dynamic process through which, in any given context, suffering and disease may be experienced and expressed. Young's definition of sickness is particularly useful in this respect:

Sickness is a process through which worrisome behavioural and biological signs, particularly ones originating in disease, are given socially recognisable meanings — they are made into symptoms and socially significant outcomes. Every culture has rules for translating signs into symptoms, for linking symptomologies to aetiologies and interventions, and for using the evidence provided by interventions to confirm translations and legitimize outcomes (Young, 1982:270).

Why is meaning so important? It is important because it is the sense that people make of events and experiences that allows them to assimilate and process their grief, anger or anxiety and thereby to heal. The anthropologist Clifford Geertz said that human experiences are formulated into a "web of meaning" abstractly defined as culture (Marcucci cited in Ledgerwood et al., 1994:129). Thus, even though the physiological experience of distress has universal characteristics, the ways in which people express and embody and give meaning to that distress is largely dependent on context — social, cultural, political and economic. The different meanings that are ascribed to catastrophic events and the manner in which people deal with stressful experiences are significantly informed by the cultural constructs and beliefs with which they are familiar. These constructs, in other words, provide a framework of understandings and beliefs which underpin the actions of individuals and the ways in which they perceive and interpret their lives. The explanations people give for violent acts and the strategies they adopt for coping, then, are in part shaped by these constructs. Making sense of a distressing experience, or at least positioning it within a world of meaning, is crucial to the process of coping and healing. By the same token, when people are unable to assimilate and comprehend painful experiences, their resilience and adjustment are affected adversely. Attributing meaning to stressful events helps reinstate order out of the chaos associated with a large scale catastrophe.

> Survivors . . . need to recreate an orderly universe. They need both to understand what it is that has happened to them and to have a sense that they now live in a structured, ordered world. They have a "heightened desire for interpretation, for finding comprehensible elements in their experience" (Myerhoff, 1978 cited in Ledgerwood et al., 1994:8).

Cultural construction of distress

To assume the universality of Western psychiatric syndromes and disorders, their signs and symptoms is, therefore, to obviate the realities of many peoples' experiences. The emphasis of the Western psychiatric approach on what happens within the individual and the search for universally applicable diagnoses and interventions at the level of the individual is divorced from cultural context and thereby offers little help in terms of understanding and assimilating responses to adversity in non-Western settings. In the Cambodian context, in which Buddhism is a defining force, the body and mind are generally conceived of as a continuum of the natural world in which both these entities are reconciled (Foong, 1995). Of course, the focus on context as mediating the experience of sickness has certain limitations since it pays little regard to the acute sufferings of individuals. In the words of a survivor of the Nazi holocaust:

> Those who did not live through the experience will never know; those who have will never tell; not really, not completely . . . the past belongs to the dead and the survivor does not recognize himself in the images and ideas which presumably depict him. . . . Auschwitz means death, total, absolute death — of man and of all people, of language and imagination, of time and of the spirit (Weisel cited in Parker, 1995).

This graphically highlights the difficulties we face in trying to comprehend and intervene in the lives of people who have been deeply affected by conflict. While there are no easy answers, it is important that we try to distance ourselves from our assumptions, think broadly and listen with great care. Such an exercise is certainly vital for institutions wishing to provide psycho-social support in post-war situations.

Similarly, to argue that individual coping and resilience is affected by broader cultural constructs is not to imply that culture constitutes a prescribed set of values and beliefs fixed in time; a set of beliefs which will predetermine people's experience of conflict and prescribe a set response. This rather static model of culture was one cherished by early anthropologists, who believed that "traditional" societies and their cultures were bounded, homogenous entities isolated from external influence. More recent thinking recognizes that cultures do not coincide neatly with the societies that they derive from and are neither bounded, nor coherent or consensual: on the contrary, they are subject to a good deal of change and contradiction. For instance, although Buddhism is a central and defining force in Cambodia, Cambodians, according to Man Hau Liev, are also influenced by Bhramanism, which, he notes, may give rise to much of the violence, long part of Cambodian society, due to associations made with the Ramayana stereotype (personal communication). That people act and believe in certain ways of doing things is based on historical adaptation and historical memory, and although there may be conservative forces within any given culture working to maintain the status quo, these are being constantly challenged and adapted in the face of "global" and other forces, external and internal. Wendy James conceives of cultural constructs not as forming, in themselves "a system or an articulated theory". She suggests rather that they are "like an archive", which:

> . . . may constitute a lasting base of past reference and future validation. They may at times rest dormant but on occasion be drawn upon for the formation of new discourse. The elements of this cultural archive, revealed as much in the repertoire of habitual ritual action as in language, constitutes the foundations of a moral world (James, 1988 cited in Allen, 1989:49).

Allen subscribes to the utility of the notion of a cultural archive because of the:

> . . . analytical advantage of something prior. It facilitates more adequate purchase on values associated with explicitly articulated 'tradition', and with the manner in which ideologies, including encoded moralities, are manufactured. It provides a frame of reference against

which 'tradition', as a reference point of thought and action, can be dismantled and discussed, rather than taken as a primordial given, or as a function of national and international political and economic forces (1989:50).

Likewise, Descola points out that most people "do not spontaneously picture their cultures as systematic wholes. Rather, they haphazardly combine partial points of view and elicited intuitions, scraps of knowledge and appeals to tradition. . . ." (Descola, 1992 cited in Kuper, 1992:10-11). Accordingly, culture is understood in this report to mean an unbounded, contested and constantly changing set of options available to people which informs and contributes to the ways in which they live, act and experience their lives on a day-to-day basis, yet does not act as a straightjacket. These options emerge out of a common past and thereby affirm the individual's membership of a given social group, as well as his or her role within it. The question of cultural meanings is particularly relevant to the Cambodian case because "cultural reform", or the elimination of existing modes of thought and practice and the enforced reinstatement of what was thought to have been a much earlier system of beliefs and values was an explicit tactic used by the Khmer Rouge during their rule to intimidate and control the civilian population. And more recently, accelerated social change associated with economic and political liberalization has been interpreted by many Cambodians and expatriates as a harbinger of cultural decay and chaos.

Locating biomedicine in other cultures

To bring into question the usefulness and validity of the biomedical model is not to say that any one model is the true model, rendering all others fictitious. Traditional healers, local community development activists and religious and political leaders all have their limitations and are not always able to provide valid explanations of catastrophe using the constructs of local cultures; nor are they necessarily able to help people suffering from serious disorders. Biomedicine is used increasingly alongside other medical systems in many parts of the world, suggesting that different models need not be mutually exclusive. Accordingly, when traditional healers are unable to contribute to healing people they often turn to Western therapies: drugs may be the only way of stabilizing people suffering from psychoses, for example.

Nevertheless, the problems associated with incorporating the biomedical tradition with other traditions need to be acknowledged. Vail (1993) illustrates, through his research in the north-east of Cambodia, how biomedical assistance being provided by a non-governmental organization (NGO) was understood and used by local communities there. He found, perhaps predictably, a mismatch between the Western medical categories and treatments and those of the indigenous medical system. The community did not, however, reject or negate the Western model but, rather, co-opted Western medicines for its own purposes.

> Kreung [healers] are subsuming Western drugs and the symptoms associated with their prescription, but they are doing so ultimately for their own culturally informed reasons. [Thus, Western] Drugs are not a cure, but they are a way to draw power from more powerful others [traditional healers and their therapies], and they contribute to potency (Vail, 1993:5).

This has significant implications for the use of psychiatry in non-Western contexts.

> The whole of medical psychology probably needs to be taught in Cambodia with a grain of salt, as the Western norms of cognitive psychology, personality theory, child

development, family systems, or social psychology, simply have not been tested in Cambodia. . . . It is probably necessary to accept as a fact of life that Cambodians will be exposed to neuropsychiatric and other psychiatric tests with no correction for the local culture (Eisenbruch, 1994).

Critics of the PTSD model, in particular, question the theoretical assumptions behind such disorders, the methods for recording their incidence as well as their relevance to non-Western societies (Bracken et al., 1995; Young, 1990; Dawes, 1992; Richman, 1992). Richman, for example, highlights the lack of diagnostic specificity of PTSD: "The symptoms comprising PTSD are only a component of the reactions experienced, and also occur in other diagnoses" (1992:6). She also draws attention to the insensitivity of the questionnaires used in diagnosis in revealing qualitative information, in that the presence of a given symptom is no indication of its extent, its severity or its impact on the child's functioning. Eisenbruch (1991a) is doubtful of the validity of PTSD diagnoses based on questionnaires that use culturally inappropriate concepts and definitions. Even if the instruments are translated and altered in some way to "fit" local cultural norms, the symptoms that are revealed by the questionnaires do not necessarily concord with traditional understandings of cause in disease and misfortune: ". . . the fact that symptoms and signs can be reliably identified in different settings is no guarantee that they mean the same thing in those settings" (Bracken et al., 1995:1074). Another problem with these different symptoms is that their presence or importance strongly depends on how they are measured (Leyens and Mahjoub, undated:30).

By locating diagnosis in individual pathology, the concept of PTSD is in direct opposition to a holistic cosmological system, such as that of Cambodia, in which aggrieved ancestors, malevolent spirits and other forces play a part in both cause and cure.

> Even a basic psychological concept such as guilt and
> responsibility . . . is linked to illness according to the
> indigenous logic of culture; the person's own ancestral
> spirits, for example, may induce mental affliction when they
> invade a person or withdraw their protection against
> spirits, and it is believed to be brought on by a lapse in
> conduct (Eisenbruch, 1994:23).

The interventions associated with a PTSD diagnosis are also seen as
problematic. When people fall ill or are distressed they generally
turn first to family and friends for assistance, both physical and
emotional. The international community often states that it aims
to support and strengthen this process, facilitating self-help
responses and trying to ensure that its interventions are compatible
with indigenous values and concepts. Working within the PTSD
framework can have virtually the opposite effect, for a number of
reasons. First, the biomedical system responds to trauma by
encouraging individuals to "talk out" their problems or undertake
drug therapy. And diagnosis and treatment are carried out by
professionals, often on a one-to-one basis. Individual therapy
conducted by an expert can isolate the sick person from his or her
family and community, undermining the efforts of neighbours and
kin to provide care. Dependence on outside technologies and
outside expertise makes it hard for families and communities to
assume control of their lives, replacing indigenous technologies,
indigenous expertise and indigenous beliefs. Nor can such
interventions be realistically sustained, for reasons of cost, and
difficulties in monitoring and follow up. Thus, in Cambodia, not
only are there very few people trained in Western psychiatry, but
as both the Khmer Buddhist Society and The Siem Riep Harvard
Programme(1) acknowledge, drugs are both difficult to obtain and

---

1   Both the Khmer Buddist Society and the Harvard programme work
      explicitly, albeit in different ways, in the field of psycho-social care.

expensive. Moreover, the equipment needed to analyse the effects of a drug on the biological functioning of the patient (which is essential to ensure that the dosage is safe) is often too costly or difficult to maintain. On the other hand, therapies that involve counselling based on a Western framework and Western concepts are problematic because they may not always be compatible with the Khmer ways of seeing things and Khmer beliefs.

Conceptualizing children and childhood

In the Western scientific tradition, childhood is conceived as a natural and universal phase of human existence, shaped more by biological and psychological than social facts (Freeman, 1993:6). These facts give prominence to children's physical and mental immaturity, and hence to their incapacities and vulnerabilities.

> Mammals are born immature and dependent. Their development and very survival depend on receiving adequate parental nurture and protection. The pattern is even more marked in human beings, who have even bigger brains and longer periods of childhood helplessness and dependency (Ingham, 1996:58).

For their own protection, nurture and enlightenment, children in Western societies are excluded from work and other such responsibilities and confined, largely, to the home and the school, where they experience a prolonged period of social immaturity and dependence. These are the conditions and circumstances that are thought to best favour children's psycho-social well-being and development. Thus, children who do not enjoy such life circumstances are believed to be at risk, their development and adaptation to society undermined.

Because it is taken for granted in this way of thinking that children have much to learn and many skills to acquire if they are to become fully responsible adults, far more attention is paid to what children do not know and cannot do than to learning about children's intrinsic strengths and capacities. This has the effect of making them seem less than adults in all respects, in terms of their cognitive, social, physical and other competencies. It also justifies an emphasis on child development and socialization, on training and preparing children for life and for society — as if they were in some way "outside" life and society. Focusing on "the route by which the finished adult mind emerges . . . preserves a privileged status for the 'finished product'" (Burman, 1994:41) and relegates childhood merely as a means to an end:

> Even the basic vocabulary of the enterprise [developmental psychology] — 'meeting needs', 'promoting intelligence', 'reaching full potential', even the word 'development' itself — reflects particular ways of thinking about the nature and goals of childhood (Woodhead, 1996:12).

It is also common in the Western scientific tradition to perceive the developmental path as a unitary process, a progression towards adult rationality, sociality, maturity and independence. In Western thinking the parameters of socialization, growth, learning and teaching are taken to be universal and it is therefore assumed that children everywhere develop along the same predetermined route, one which can be assessed in standardized behavioural and developmental tests (Woodhead, 1990).

These are ideas that have many implications for the theoretical understanding of childhood and for action to support children experiencing psycho-social distress. There are some serious shortcomings with this approach. For one thing, theories of child development founded on the notion of growing adequacy and competence in children disguise the unique capacities of children and at the same time render childhood insignificant, as Schildkrout notes:

> . . . while there has been an increasing concern with childhood as something distinct from adulthood, the emphasis on socialization has trivialized childhood as a social status. Children rarely enter descriptions of social systems, any more than they enter the system of production . . . (Schildkrout, 1978:110).

Another area of contention is the way in which "deviations" in child development are perceived. Children living outside the parameters of "normal development" are understood to be at disproportionate risk of developmental impairment or some other kind of damage. This includes children exposed to political violence or other extreme circumstances. But despite the extensive range of possible adverse psycho-social effects, children are not passive in the face of adversities such as violence and a high proportion remain astonishingly resilient even under the most difficult situations (Turton et al., 1991; Zwi et al., 1992). Indeed, there is strong evidence that in most conflicts only a small minority of children exposed suffer serious long-term mental health problems (Cairns, 1996:33). It is normal to manifest acute emotional reactions following a highly stressful event. But in most cases severe anxiety reactions are short term, and, with time, the majority of children overcome and find ways of coping with stress (Rutter, 1994; Gibson, 1989).

The idea of a unitary process of development also belies the very different experiences and expectations of childhood associated with differences in social status. As psychologist Martin Woodhead argues: "The territory of childhood is marked by numerous pathways to development" (1990:95) and children in different cultures and social settings grow and flourish within a broad range of child-rearing traditions and parental belief systems. A great diversity of conceptions of childhood, linked with gender, birth order and distinctions of class, ethnicity or religion and urban or rural origin can coexist even within one society. There may also be major differences between children based on physical endowment, health, personality and other individual attributes. Seldom are all children equally esteemed and the personal and social structural distinctions that shape each child's identity have a crucial bearing on its life chances and childhood experiences. Indeed, in many contexts, the divisions and power within childhood have greater bearing than the larger division between child and adult.

The physical and emotional dependency of infants and young children everywhere is an undisputable fact. But the error is to link uncritically children's extended social dependence in the West with notions of weakness and incapacity. Many of the attributes and weaknesses of children are socially, rather than physiologically, ascribed: many societies do not agree with Western notions but view even quite young children as having attributes that can be harnessed and used for the good of the wider social group. Unlike Western children, children in many other parts of the world participate actively in productive activities, household chores and the care of younger children.

Of course, younger children are generally given fewer responsibilities than older ones. Often the transitions in social status and roles within childhood are marked formally by rites of passage. In these popular accounts of child development there appear some broad global features. The first social transition often takes place at around age six, with the end of early childhood and the beginning of the middle childhood years. Children frequently begin to work seriously at about this age and may be punished more severely for misbehaviour. They may be required to observe new codes of dress and social behaviour: in highly differentiated and hierarchical societies, the rules of avoidance between males and females frequently begin to apply at this point (Schildkrout, 1978). Another critical age threshold falls around 12 to 14 years, when children (especially girls) are given substantially increased work responsibilities and are at risk of dropping out of school — if they have ever attended — and when, in some cases, girls particularly become eligible for marriage.

Many societies, then, hold a view of child socialization and development which is very different from that of the West: central to this view is the idea that children learn and develop by participating in rather than being protected from social and economic processes. This idea is expressed in attitudes towards children's work, which is frequently thought by parents, children and employers to ensure learning and social integration.

The rights and responsibilities assigned to different categories of children at different stages in their lives may also critically influence their experience of violence and the impacts such experience has on their lives. This point is graphically illustrated by Ray McGrath, based on work he conducted in northern Iraq/Kurdistan (personal communication). Here, the gender division of labour assigns girls the role of collecting firewood and boys the task of herding animals. Because the forests and pastures are mined, both activities entail serious risk but the pattern of risk is not even, since girls are at particular risk in the autumn and winter, when the collection of firewood is at its peak, and boys are more likely to be affected during the spring, when the snows melt and the livestock are taken to fresh pastures.

In some societies bearing arms, or assuming an active role in combat, plays an essential part in the transitions boys undergo during childhood. This is the case among the Samburu of East Africa, for example, who adhere to a complicated series of age sets and age grades by which the growing maturity and responsibility of boys is publicly acknowledged (Gilmore, 1990). Likewise, among the Sambia, Gisu and Mende, boys become men by passing exacting tests of performance in war, economic pursuits and procreativity. In such contexts the involvement of boys in violence is socially validated, making the transition from traditional warrior, wielding a bow and arrows or spear, to modern fighter, bearing a rifle, very straightforward.

These powerful social attitudes play a vital role in influencing the ways in which children engage with and are affected by violence: their appraisal and assessment is thus essential in any study of the psycho-social impacts of political violence, bringing into question the value of research which focuses on the individual experience alone (Ben-Ezer, 1990; Dawes, 1992; Dawes and Tredoux, 1989). Accordingly, discussions of the involvement of Palestinian children in the Intifada and black South African children in the anti-apartheid movement have dwelt on the question of whether possible adverse psycho-social consequences can be mitigated by a common commitment to a political cause: the point being that these children, like the young Gisu and Mende warriors, receive social approval for what they do and are defined as heroes rather than villains or victims. A few authors (for example, Baker, 1990) have suggested that youths could even gain emotionally or psychologically from active and voluntary participation in combat. This, however, depends very much on their position in relation to the events, as we describe in the following chapter.

PART 2

Mediating Vulnerability and Resilience in Cambodia

Street children playing at the railway station in Phnom Penh.
Credit: Peter Williams/WCC Photo.

2.1

The History of Violence

Twenty-five years of Cambodia's past: From crisis to crisis

It is important to establish, as far as possible, the actual conditions or circumstances that have affected Cambodian children in recent history, since this helps to ascertain the degree of possible threat to their psycho-social well-being. There are many kinds of conflict and many ways in which children and families experience conflict. People often think of wounding and death as being the main problem, because these are the most direct and obvious consequences of violence. However, military engagement is but one strategy of combat and one kind of stressor. Just as armed conflict has many different kinds of stressor, so it has many different kinds of impact: ecological, physical, material, psychological and social: some of these impacts are structural, others personal.

Indeed, many of the most grave consequences of conflict are not physical. This is especially true of conflicts in which control of the civilian population is achieved by means of systematic social engineering, and the undermining of civilian structures and processes through psychological warfare, forced labour and other such tactics. Adverse structural consequences include the dislocation of social institutions and attack on religious beliefs and values. Because of the mediating role of such structural forces in personal coping, damage to family and community networks or prohibition of religious observance and other such phenomena can cause serious problems for children, whether in terms of mental health, social or moral development, or social distress.

The specificity and form of the violent event(s) have an important bearing on psycho-social and physical well-being. What kind of event(s), for example, have children in Cambodia been exposed to? In recent history, the country has undergone several devastating political, social and economic emergencies. Political violence has been widespread since the 1960s. But the severity of violence and social upheaval has always varied considerably from one region to another and while some parts of the country have experienced peace since 1979, others have been subjected to continuous, if low-intensity, violence. To understand Cambodia today, one needs to appreciate the different impacts of these past disruptions and also to take into account the differences in experiences of civilians from different social groups living in different parts of the country. Overall, the most intensive and consistent violence has taken place in the northern and western provinces.

Conflict in Cambodia has been influenced by and shaped according to a series of political "régimes", as follows (UNICEF, 1995).

The Kingdom of Cambodia: 1953 - 1970

After independence in 1953, Cambodia slowly prospered and developed under the highly centralized leadership of Prince Norodom Sihanouk. Although poorer than neighbouring countries, by the late 1960s Cambodia had become a net exporter of rice, almost self-sufficient in basic foodstuffs. Economic growth was short lived, though, as the country became embroiled in the Viet Nam war towards the end of the 1960s when the Americans started a blanket bombing of the eastern provinces, through which the Viet Cong had been transporting arms.

The Khmer Republic: 1970 - 1975

In 1970, Prince Sihanouk was ousted from government by General Lon Nol, with the backing of the United States, and the Prince joined forces with the Khmer Rouge. Between 1969 and 1973 the United States dropped an estimated 550,000 tons of bombs on Cambodia (Mysliwiec, 1988:2). These bombings, together with the guerrilla activities of the period, left hundreds of thousands of people dead and similar numbers uprooted and internally displaced, many fleeing from the countryside to refugee camps around the cities. By the time the Khmer Rouge took power in 1975, more than a million displaced people had taken refuge in shelters around Phnom Penh.

"Democratic Kampuchea"(1): 1975 - 1979

On 19 April 1975, the Khmer Rouge initiated what is widely known as one of the most savage and brutal periods of rule in modern international history. This period represented the most acute crisis in Cambodia's recent past, associated not only with extreme violence but also extensive social engineering and economic dis-

---

1   Democratic Kampuchea, rather ironically, was the name that the Khmer Rouge gave to the country during their far from democratic period of rule.

ruption. An army of approximately 60,000 combatants seized control of the country and in four years was responsible for the deaths of between one and two million people.

Most Cambodians who are aged 35 or over today have witnessed the deaths of family and friends by execution, torture, starvation, disease or exhaustion, and have also experienced forced migration and dissolution of family and religion. They have also seen the deliberate destruction of their economy and their educational and health care systems as they were known before 1968. The human and institutional damage wrought by the Khmer Rouge régime prolonged and broadened the destruction that had taken place between 1968 and 1975 (UNICEF, 1995).

It was the explicit aim of the Khmer Rouge to fashion Democratic Kampuchea after the ancient Angkor society(2). Songs drew parallels between the glories of the Khmer Rouge régime and those of Angkor times, and Khmer Rouge attempts to radically redesign the irrigation system nationally were consistent with the idea that irrigation was the basis of the glories of Angkor.

> The Pol Pot régime made a conscious attempt to sever the usual bonds of allegiance and trust which bind a society together. . . . The society was systematically dismembered . . . All the usual means of socialization were removed or undermined (Taylor, 1994:28).

---

2   The zenith of the ancient Angkor society was between the ninth and thirteenth centuries.

Control was exerted in the name of Angka, the obscure and yet omnipresent Khmer Rouge revolutionary organization. A Khmer metaphor, "Angka has the eyes of a pineapple", captures the sense of fear instilled by the organization. "Briefly stated, it means that the revolutionary organization, Angka, knows everything that is going on — it can see in all directions, just as the eyes of the pineapple point in all directions" (Marston, 1994:114-5). People were admonished that they should not break rules or resist authority because "Angka has the eyes of a pineapple" and would know whatever they did.

But social reconstruction went further still, intending to change the ways in which people thought, acted and related to each other:

> Conformity was obtained particularly through the regulation of bodily movement, the body thus becoming a tool for the exercise of political control. People were not only forced to look alike, with identical clothes and haircuts, but also to talk, eat and sleep in a standardized manner. Communal eating, standardized clothing, linguistic alterations such as general terms of address which made no distinction between age or sex, and the demolition of large houses were some of the methods to standardize village life. To ensure compliance the body was also used as an instrument of punishment, being literally beaten into obedience (Uimonen, 1994:6).

People were told to "build themselves" *(kasang khluon)*. Cambodians today use expressions such as "did they ever *kasang* you [in the Pol Pot period]?" in the sense of being "reconstructed" (Uimonen, 1994:6).

The People's Republic of Kampuchea: 1979 - 1989
In 1979, The People's Republic of Kampuchea (PKR) was established with the backing of Vietnamese troops, the Khmer Rouge having been overthrown from their seat in Phnom Penh. A massive emergency

operation was carried out between 1979 and 1982 with short-lived assistance from the West. Due to the lack of international support and the serious physical and human resource deficiencies, economic recovery in Cambodia was extremely slow. Nevertheless, services were gradually re-established throughout the country and in a series of centrally-planned measures, state-owned enterprises made an important contribution to the economy. In the mid-1980s, a process of market-oriented restructuring was introduced, although this was weakened by poor implementation, lack of technical and financial support from overseas and the allocation of a large proportion of available resources for military purposes.

During this time 350,000 refugees remained in camps on the Thai border. From among their number a three party coalition that included the Khmer Rouge was formed. This coalition was recognized internationally as the legitimate government of Cambodia.

The State of Cambodia: 1989 - 1991
The PKR was reorganized and reformed in 1989 to make way for the end of Cambodia's isolation. Vietnamese troops withdrew and Buddhism was reinstated, together with the market economy. This liberalization facilitated the Paris Peace Accords of 1991, which in turn led to a transitional period and the United Nations-supervised election of 1993.

UNTAC and The Supreme National Council: 1991 - 1993
The transition and election were overseen by the United Nations Transitional Authority in Cambodia (UNTAC), together with the Supreme National Council (SNC). The latter was made up of the three resistance factions from the border camps and the former State of Cambodia government. The operation began early in 1992 when, after years of isolation from the international community, more than 20,000 military and civilian peace-keeping personnel were sent to Cambodia. Lasting 21 months and costing more than 2 billion dollars, the aim of

the UN operation was to oversee the peace process and promote post-conflict reconstruction and rehabilitation. Although the UNTAC mission facilitated some important achievements and has been heralded internationally as a major success, it also caused many problems. Certainly it brought an end to Cambodia's isolation and provided access to foreign aid and technical assistance. It also had the effect of stimulating trade, private enterprise, construction and infrastructural repairs, generating employment and promoting training (UNRISD, 1993). The repatriation of more than 360,000 refugees from Thailand was another key development and the programme of electoral education and registration was a remarkable achievement, especially given the many security constraints.

When a country is undergoing a process of transition and is suddenly opened up to numerous international agencies and personnel there are likely to be difficulties. And given the complexity of the Cambodian situation the task was inevitably fraught with problems (Utting, 1994). Thus, although many of the refugees were repatriated, the numbers of internally displaced had increased by the time the UNTAC personnel left the country. Moreover, even though the election heralded a period of comparative stability politically, a lasting peace was not secured. The Khmer Rouge gained more control over national territory (with assistance from Thailand) and the levels of conflict between the Khmer Rouge and the State of Cambodia to some extent escalated (Jennar, April 1994).

There were other problems. The host population was marginalized in key decision-making processes during the UNTAC operation and essential public services and community institutions were further weakened. That the aid budget was earmarked for short-term humanitarian relief only, when such aid detracts from longer term development assistance, did little to build local capacities. And aid was targeted to a relatively small percentage of the population in need (Utting, 1994).

The majority of what is essentially an agrarian population experienced increased hardship. The massive expenditures deriving from the salaries and per diems of UNTAC personnel and staff members of 100 international organizations reached several hundred million US dollars, distorting the economy and contributing to inflation (UNRISD, 1993). Inflation and the competition between the international agencies and UNTAC for housing and local labour caused a diversion of investment away from essential services and towards facilities and services required by the international community. Public sector workers sought employment with international agencies and private sector bodies, seriously undermining education and health care. "Furthermore, it involved a process of "de-professionalization" — cases, for example, of doctors or medical assistants abandoning their areas of specialization to work as translators or drivers" (Utting, 1994:10).

The influx of foreign UNTAC personnel also brought an increase in social distress, due partly to the fact that many of the people deployed to Cambodia had very little understanding of the country's recent history and circumstances. Jennar (September 1992) notes that no pre-deployment studies were carried out (which could have seriously reduced the cost of the operation) and that the impact of the UNTAC operation on Cambodian society was monitored hardly at all.

> There has been an increase in lawlessness, banditry, corruption, xenophobic tensions and violence; a sharp growth in prostitution and the incidence of HIV/AIDS infection; a rise in the number of street children; and a further deterioration in the situation of vulnerable groups, which now include segments of the returnee population (UNRISD, 1993:19).

The image of the peace-keeping operation was undermined in Cambodia by poor relations with the host population and disrespect

for its customs. The most serious example of this was
harassment of women by some UNTAC personnel. T₁
escalation in prostitution led to a tenfold increase in the incide
HIV/AIDS infections in 1992 alone. An increase in the numbe₁
children in the sex industry was also noted and is thought to have been
associated with minimizing the risk to clients of HIV infection
(UNRISD, 1993).

Kingdom of Cambodia: 1993 - present

The UNTAC period passed, as some Cambodians have remarked:
"like a dust storm . . . it stirred things up and now that the dust has
settled you would never know it had happened" (NGO worker). But
the lessons to be learned from the operation are relevant today, since
there remains a large international presence in the country. Thus:

> Above all . . . [there is] a need for the international community
> to pause and reflect upon the implications [of their
> interventions] for economic and social development and on
> the way it goes about the business of peace-making and
> rehabilitating war-torn societies (UNRISD, 1993:25).

In 1993, a new coalition government was formed alongside the
reinstated constitutional monarchy headed by Prince Norodom
Sihanouk. Despite many advances in recent years, a number of serious
problems remain. Military expenditure is rising and military activity
still disrupts civilian life. In May 1994, a large military offensive left
50,000 people displaced, many of whom were unable to return home
because of landmines or continued hostilities. As one expatriate aid
worker commented: "This is not a 'post' situation — security problems
are still very much alive here".

Significant tracts of the countryside remain under Khmer Rouge
control and civilians continue to be caught in the crossfire. In parts of
Battambang province, for example, farmers are unable to work in the

fields after 3 p.m. because of fighting. The laying of landmines persists and their widespread presence in certain provinces seriously affects access to land, thereby reducing livelihood, as well as causing death and injury. Banditry is a serious problem in some areas. Weapons abound among civilians and combatants alike and are carried about freely, even in Phnom Penh. The violence is not generalized, but all the same Cambodia can best be described as a country experiencing low-intensity conflict rather than as a post-conflict or transitional society. Indeed, in some areas conflict has become institutionalized: "It is true that the war changed our society but society is now causing the war to go on. If people can't get jobs they go to the forest and the fighting continues" (teacher in Battambang Province).

After over two decades of conflict and isolation Cambodia remains one of the poorest countries in the world, with a GDP estimated at only US \$ 200 per capita and a very poor income distribution. Severe degradation of the natural environment, due partly to the timber and logging activities of unregulated extractive industries and partly to the dissemination of landmines, forcing population concentrations into safe areas, is having a devastating effect on fishing and farming in some regions. Lack of access to productive resources, credit, technology and information and decision-making processes exacerbates poverty and powerlessness, which are in turn associated with widespread exploitation, civil strife and outbreaks of violence (Working Group on Aid Co-ordination, 1995). Indeed,

> [t]here is evidence to suggest that large sectors of the popu-
> lation are more vulnerable today than at any time since the
> Pol Pot era, while the capacity of the Cambodian state to
> regulate the process of rehabilitation and reconstruction has
> been considerably weakened (UNRISD, undated).

The characteristics of catastrophic experiences

Social and cultural context may shape human experience in a way that is critical to psycho-social resilience and vulnerability, but stressful experiences come in many different forms: it is not just the social meanings given to violent or catastrophic events that influence responses, because the objective characteristics of such experiences also mediate impact. Conflict may be extremely intense but short-lived, for example; or it may be drawn out over many years, though involving civilians only intermittently. Equally, children may experience a whole range of stressful events, or just one.

> Dramatic traumas such as torture or severe abuse are more obvious, but children are also distressed by such insidious traumas as the lack of parental nurture and care, living with abusive parents . . . and family break-ups due to the parents' own traumas. . . . As reported among Afghan refugees, causes of psycho-social stresses include such physical stresses as a long hot season with poor sanitation and insufficient drinking water; lack of educational opportunity; separation from important love objects; anxiety disorders and depressive reactions of parents; and such stresses as unemployment, family break-up, changes in social hierarchy, absences of fathers, humiliation and lack of respect (Ressler et al., 1992:170-171, referring also to Dafar 1988:34).

Ressler et al. note how it is seldom that well-adjusted, well-cared-for children are suddenly overwhelmed by a singular traumatic experience. They remind us that of those children who suffer psycho-social distress a significant proportion have not been subject to major traumatic experiences but to less dramatic circumstances that are deleterious or unfulfilling: "More often children and adults exhibiting distress in conflict situations will have endured a series of hardships and deprivations accentuated by particularly difficult circumstances"

(1988:171). They go on to outline a framework which characterizes catastrophic or debilitating experiences for their potential to cause psycho-social distress in children. Certain key features of a stressful experience are seen as associated with psycho-social risk, as follows:

The nature of stressful experiences is important because traumatic events may be experienced "in many ways — as specific very severe incidents, such as bombardment, loss of loved ones or the slow insidious traumas of displacement, poverty, disruption of social support and pervasive fear" (ibid.:178-179).

The **severity** of an event "can vary from minor inconvenience to life-shattering alteration" (ibid.:179) and refers to the degree of physical, social, mental and economic disturbance, but is hard to ascribe since it is a fairly subjective criterion and is not an automatic predictor of distress. No one can doubt the overwhelming impact of the Khmer Rouge period, in that lives were disrupted — in many cases destroyed — communities fractured and the economy devastated. This is the period in the country's history that preoccupies the Cambodian people most today.

Distribution is the number of traumatic experiences a child is exposed to. This is significant because exposure to a number of events, such as displacements or violent acts, can have a cumulative psycho-social effect. This point was reinforced by the leader of a village in Battambang province:

> Each time those [internally displaced] people have fled the fighting they have lost a lot. When they come here, they lose everything there and when they go back there, they lose everything here. All this coming and going, each time people lose more and more (Phum leader/traditional healer).

Many Cambodians have suffered repeatedly a range of stressful events. Take, for example, the refugees who lived in the camps along the Thai border. If the appalling circumstances of their flight were not bad enough, exile in the camps made things much worse, leading to high rates of suicide and attempted suicide, depression and other major psycho-social problems:

> The conditions in the Thai camps believed to be responsible for causing serious mental illness included lack of physical safety, ongoing violence, overcrowding, and malnutrition. . . . Families lived in fear of physical harm and were threatened with chronic hunger and malnutrition because of the escalation in human rights violations by the Khmer military (Mollica et al., 1994:91).

Aggregation refers to the extent to which a traumatic experience is shared by others. "For some children commonly shared experiences may be less traumatic than experiences they suffer alone" (Ressler, op.cit.:179-180). This point has special relevance for Cambodia since, as Thion powerfully stated, the violence and devastation wrought by successive political forces on the Khmer people ruined the lives of millions and yet at the same time "seems to remain circumscribed in personal history" (Thion, 1993:181). As we shall see later, there is much discussion and debate in Cambodia today about the rise of individualism and lack of trust as a consequence of both culture and conflict, and it is suggested by some that the Khmer suffer more by not being able to share their grief with others.

The **speed of onset** of the event is also a variable, in the sense that children and adults are likely to cope better with slow-onset events. With sudden catastrophes there is little time to anticipate, assimilate or prepare for an emergency. Thus, for example, many adult Cambodians today hold vivid and disturbing memories of the shock they felt on 19 April 1975, when the Khmer Rouge entered Phnom Penh and ordered all civilians to leave the city; none were prepared for, and few were able to deal with, the horrors that were to follow.

Duration of a stressful experience is another key contributor in children's responses. A number of studies (for example, McCallin, 1991) emphasize the debilitating effect on children of drawn-out situations of violence or turmoil. Certainly the Cambodian emergency has been long term, extending over more than two decades and affecting generations of children and adults. Of course, duration is not necessarily a reliable predictor of impact, because the longer a situation endures, the more it can become routine and commonplace. The "normalization" of violence or other potentially stressful events over long periods is a major issue in the debate about moral and political learning in children, in that some suggest (and others dispute) that the experience of violence as a normal and routine event in childhood begets violence in adulthood. Related to this latter issue is the **predictability** of an experience. "Predictable events are easier to respond to than those that appear random or unpredictable" (Ressler, op.cit.:180), although predictability can lead children to become nonchalant in the face of fighting, bombing and death, and this can be hazardous. In keeping with the thinking of other psychologists such as Dawes and Ben-Ezer, Ressler et al. (1992) comment that **explainability**, or an objective and subjective understanding, of stressful events is an important variable in psycho-social well-being of children. As the discussion in Part 1 indicated, this is an issue of central importance to the present paper.

Children's position in relation to stressful events

Ressler et al. argue that a catastrophic event is likely to have very different effects on children depending upon whether they are personally targeted, secondary victims, perpetrators or simply observers of violence. Possibly the majority of children in situations of conflict are secondary victims or observers, in that their suffering is a result of events such as damage to the family economy or to family unity, or the death and violence of relatives and friends. However, countless children in Cambodia's recent history are direct victims of conflict, having been wounded, tortured or killed, or become sick or died of starvation or exhaustion.

Even those who were not harmed physically were unlikely to escape altogether. From the late 1960s through the early 1970s, for example, hundreds of thousands of children and their families were displaced as a result of both the American bombing and the fighting between the insurgents and Lon Nol. Cambodian aid worker Meas Nee, recalling his childhood, mentions how the battles raging on the Vietnamese border could be heard from his village and how later, when the fighting reached the village, he was separated from his family. He remembers the fear and confusion about which side they were expected to support and how they were forced to leave their home, never to return (Meas with Healy, 1995).

Many other children have participated directly in combat. One of the features of the Khmer Rouge rule was that children were actively drawn into the violence as instruments of the régime. They were crucially involved in the revolution at all levels: in the economy; in the fighting; and in carrying out repressive or violent acts against civilians. Spy units, *Kang Chhlop*, composed mainly of children, for example, were used to report what the communes said to the Angkar (Duffy, 1994).

In the Pol Pot times children could catch an adult if they thought they had done wrong. They could beat the adult. For example, if an adult was caught stealing fruit a child could tell the soldiers: "look they are our enemies". Then the soldiers would set a chair for the child to stand on so that they [sic] could beat the adult's head (Khmer woman working for an international NGO).

A 1973 Khmer Rouge document, translated by Timothy M. Carney, says that:

. . . the party has educated, watched, nourished, and re-educated youth as the central force in the revolutionary movement of each era and as the central force for future national reconstruction . . . (Carney cited in Marston, 1994:113).

Several researchers internationally have focused on the moral and psychological impact on children of direct participation in violence, although the evidence for Cambodia is lacking. Some (for example, Boothby et al., 1991) argue that when children engage directly in fighting this has a more severe impact on psycho-social welfare and development than being involved as a victim. As previously noted this is again dependent upon the child's positioning: adverse impact is less obvious among children who fight voluntarily for a common political cause than it is among those conscripted into an army whose ideals they do not share.

2.2

Social and Economic Factors Mediating Impact

Since the pioneering work of Freud and Burlingham in England after the Second World War, it has been widely accepted that strong social networks and mechanisms of social support can mediate the effect on children of organized violence. At the heart of these networks lies the family (however defined), the primary social unit in all societies and the unit normally responsible for the nurture and care of children. Indeed, the mental and physical state of the parent or prime caregiver has often been understood as the single most important factor in children's coping in the context of conflict. But children's welfare is not just dependent on the family, nor even on their own inner resources, since the wider network of neighbours, friends and relatives in the extended kinship group can also play an important role — possibly all the more so in "traditional" rural societies. And among older children and adolescents in particular, peer groups also have considerable influence on psycho-social well-being.

Arguably the most severe impact of the last 25 years of conflict in Cambodia has been the serious disruption to normal civilian life. The Khmer Rouge period was particularly devastating in this regard. While they may have gained notoriety internationally for their brutality and for the large number of deaths that occurred during their reign, their efforts to reconstruct Cambodian society and culture, to rewrite its history, eradicate its social structures, beliefs and values, could ultimately have more lasting adverse effect. Certainly the consequences of this endeavour still shadow the lives of Cambodian children today, since it undermined both the collective and individual psyche, leaving many adults — now parents, grandparents, aunts and uncles — hurt in one way or another. That said, it is also remarkable how many people in Cambodia have been able to forge a life for themselves and their families despite the difficult circumstances. These coping strategies also bear analysis if aid interventions are to help build resilience further, for the most effective interventions are likely to be those that consolidate and reinforce existing resources rather than deploy new ones. Indeed, referring to conflict in the African context, Tim Allen remarks that;

> Shallow analyses, and the mixing of descriptions of barbarism and helplessness, with ethno-centric moralizing, or partial critiques of relief and development programmes, do not bring us any closer to answering the question: How do people manage to maintain, and persistently reconstruct, viable ways of life? Surely that is the most important question in micro-level analysis of disasters in Africa: not what happens when so many people suffer terribly and die (if indeed they do)? (Allen, 1989:47).

The challenge, therefore, is to identify those structural features of Cambodian society that underpin individual and group resilience and coping.

Cambodian social classifications

Who people perceive as their friends and who they identify as potential or actual enemies have crucial bearing on vulnerability and coping in the face of adversity, as do the various roles and responsibilities assigned to different members of society; and in a hierarchical society like Cambodia, even who you have as patron may affect survival — hence the importance of social analysis to assessments of resilience in countries affected by political violence. Ovesen et al. (1995:14) describe the fundamental classifications that order the Cambodian social world today. The indigenous categories they identify express the social distinctions that the Khmer recognize as important in guiding relations between groups and individuals. They estimate that about 85 per cent of the population consists of farming peasants, who can be divided into two, sometimes overlapping, categories; *neak sre* and *neak chamkar*. *Neak* means person and *sre*, rice field, and the majority of the population falls in this category, "the people of the rice fields", which is constituted of subsistence paddy-farmers. The *neak chamkar*, or riverside farmers, grow rice, maize, beans and other crops on the fertile banks of Cambodia's major rivers.

Urban dwellers, *neak krong*, constitute a third category:

> They are the small, more or less educated middle class whom
> the peasants treat with a mixture of respect and suspicion
> because they are the ones who 'eat the country' rather than
> cultivate the fields, and because they are associated with city

life which is in many ways felt incompatible, or at least at variance with, traditional Khmer cultural ideas and values. (Ovesen et al., 1995:14).

The *barang*, or foreigners, represent a fourth category. They are perceived in a similar light as the *neak krong*, although because of their association with development aid and economic gain are perhaps viewed more positively. Consisting of indigenous tribal minorities that live largely by swidden agriculture in the hills in the northern and eastern provinces, the *neak prey*, forest people, exist on the margins of Khmer society and are regarded by the Khmer as inferior. Potentially dangerous, the *neak ta*, "ancient ones", are the spirits: perceived as "real living persons", Ovesen et al. maintain, not strictly ancestral spirits in the sense that they represent specific deceased relatives, but rather the "personifications of the common territory of the family or group, spirits of the land" (1995:15).

> That the *neak ta* are indeed living persons with histories and destinies comparable to those of humans is evinced by the fact that they not only suffered greatly, but even were sometimes defeated at the hand of Pol Pot (1995:15).

Ovesen et al. confirmed the status of *neak ta* as living beings during their fieldwork, when one spirit became an internally displaced person when it was not repatriated with the villagers who recognized it but remained alone and distressed in the mountains in the north of Siem Reap.

In addition to these classifications there are important differences based on ethnicity: in fact, ethnicity has been one of the key distinctions in Cambodia out of which political violence has grown. The great majority of Cambodians, probably over 90 per cent, are ethnic Khmer (Ovesen et al., 1995:21). There are in addition some 30 indigenous minorities based in the hilly areas, although together they make up no more than 3 per cent of the total population. Most of these minorities speak languages falling in the Mon-Khmer family.

There is a largely urban Chinese population in Cambodia, concentrated mainly in the commercial sector. While the Chinese have mostly been assimilated into Khmer society, the Vietnamese are perceived very much as outsiders and are little liked, especially among the urban middle class. Viet Nam has long been perceived by Cambodians as a threat to their sovereignty, and the Vietnamese living in Cambodia have been subjected at different points in history to serious discrimination, which, during the Pol Pot era, escalated to an overt policy of ethnocide.

Cambodia is an extremely hierarchical society and age and gender are the two central distinctions at the individual level that, although cross-cut by other important distinctions of social status, govern all social relations:

> People usually refer to one another by kinship terminology which reflects the age and sex of the person who is referenced. This is only relative though, and symbolic markers also include a range of other factors such as wealth, reputation of family, political position, employment, the character of the individual, and religious piety (Ovesen et al., 1995:40, referring to Ledgerwood, 1992).

In research in the village of West Svay conducted between 1959 and 1960, anthropologist May Ebihara studied the ageing process for differences in roles and status in the life cycle (Ebihara, 1968). There are many parallels in the patterns of development and socialization between children in this village and in other non-Western societies: for one thing, work clearly played a vital role. Ebihara found that infants and young children *(kon)* were indulged and protected and spent most of their time in the company of their mother. Illegitimate children were called *kon prey*, children of the wilderness, because lovers would usually seek deserted areas to have sexual relations. It is not clear whether illegitimate children were stigmatized or neglected. The relationship with the mother became less close and less indulgent at the birth of a sibling or at age five. At this stage children began to associate more frequently with their peers, playing or carrying out light chores. At about six or seven children of both sexes would begin to collect firewood, one of the most important daily activities in rural areas, and also to attend school. This was the age when gender distinctions began to emerge in the division of labour, with girls taking care of younger siblings. By about age 10, girls would cook the family meal, while boys would be out tending cattle.

At one time the transition to adolescence, at about age 13, was marked in West Svay by elaborate rites. But these died out some time before Ebihara undertook her study and by the 1960s there was no longer a clear-cut demarcation between childhood and adolescence. Even so, age 16 was recognized as an important time of transition; young people of this age were considered to be on the threshold of adulthood and were no longer referred to as children but as *kromom* (unmarried female) and *krolaa* (unmarried male). Nevertheless, the passage into full social adulthood was marked only by marriage. With this end in view, adolescents would take an increasingly active role in household and subsistence tasks, assuming gender-linked tasks. Adolescents could also work to earn money, participate in ceremonial activity, and express concern for earning merit and fear of incurring the retribution of spirits.

Gender inequity in Cambodia has traditionally assigned women an inferior status to men: "the wife calls her husband *bong* [elder] even if he is younger than she is" (Martin, 1994 cited in Ovesen et al., 1995:10). Ebihara notes in her study of West Svay that, according to the legal code, the man was defined as head of the family, although women had considerable authority in many areas of life and could initiate divorce proceedings and own and dispose of property in their own right. Also, the gender division of labour was less pronounced than in some other countries in the region. Older women in particular would hold a position of some of importance, since the elderly were generally awarded much respect.

Family support

The most powerful affective ties during childhood originate within the family and the family can be a vital source of confidence, trust and support for children. The family is also the most important determinant of social status and wealth in individuals, as well being the primary unit of socialization. Ebihara states that in Cambodia close kin, especially parents, siblings or children, were almost always the first people to be called upon in times of need, contributing their labour, lending, donating, and participating in life-cycle and other ceremonies. Ties were particularly strong among maternal relatives.

Psychological resilience is greatly influenced by the amount of care and nurture children receive, in infancy and early childhood especially. Richman et al. (1989), for example, emphasize the persisting effects of past experiences among Mozambican children. Children respond to new experiences in part on the basis of what has happened to them in the past and so, for example, those who have benefited since infancy from nurturing care can draw upon that experience and deal more effectively with adversity than those who have not. The ability of family members or other important reference persons to provide consistent care, or a stable, nurturing environment is fundamental to children's coping during adversity and will depend very much on the personal and social circumstances of its various members. It has already been suggested that disunity, separation, ill health, poverty, abuse and other problems within the family seriously undermine resilience in children.

Families are often unable to remain independent and resilient in the context of conflict, and a weakened family structure poses a direct threat to children's welfare.

A lot is said about the poor quality of family life in Cambodia today. This is a theme discussed especially among expatriate aid workers. The information on family life prior to the 1970s derives mainly from Ebihara's study of West Svay. But this was limited, in that the research was conducted in a particular area which may well not be representative and did not cover many of the qualitative aspects of domestic organization and family relations (Ebihara, 1968). The marked absence of research on intra-familial relations, and the quality of family life generally, prior to the outbreak of war makes recent assertions in research about increases in domestic violence in Cambodia due to conflict difficult to substantiate. Because of this lack of longitudinal data, it is not even possible to prove with any confidence that the high proportion of female headed and female managed households in Cambodia today is directly attributable to the decades of violence and social deterioration, an assertion made in several studies.

Nevertheless, even without systematic information it is evident that the family and household have traditionally been the only enduring and clearly defined social units in Cambodia. Ebihara comments that the villagers would generally distrust and fear any place where they had no kin or friends. Most rural communities at this time originated in a cluster of households of close kin, growing through the constant addition of new homes established by successive generations of married children and other relatives. Many households contained stem or extended families in one form or another. Like the Thai system, the Khmer kinship system is cognatic, although the Khmer seem to attach greater importance than the Thais to the nuclear family and the focal couple. Ovesen et al. remark on "the absence among the Khmer of formally structured, functional kin groups beyond the nuclear family.

Even solidarity between parents and married children is not institutionally formalized, and cannot be taken for granted in all situations" (Ovesen et al., 1995:40). The mutual rights and obligations of family members and the nature of the relations between them were defined and sanctioned by legal statutes in the civil code, by Buddhist precepts and teachings, by belief in ancestral spirits — who oversaw their descendant's conduct — and by general cultural norms regarding proper behaviour within the family.

An assessment of psycho-social vulnerability in Cambodian children today would need to take into account the evidence for family breakdown and separation, adult (parental) mortality and abandonment and other such phenomena. Loss of a parent or key carer and difficulties in the relationship with new carers are common consequences of political violence. Because of stress among adults, some children may simply lose their parent's attention and this can also be very devastating. Punamaki (1987), for example, found the most consistent correlate of psychological disorders in children to be depression in mothers and mothers' pessimistic appraisal of their lives and family status. Similarly, McCallin (1991) established that the more difficulties displaced mothers encountered in their own experiences, the more problems they reported in connection with their children's behaviour.

It is often extremely difficult for families to remain together during conflict, and many children become separated from their parents, although separation occurs more often during flight from fighting than in the actual zone of conflict. As a very rough measure, some 2 to 5 per cent of all displaced and refugee children globally are unaccompanied (Williamson and Moser, 1987). It is generally assumed that unaccompanied children constitute one of the most vulnerable groups in situations of organized violence, since they tend to be isolated from services, and family and community support mechanisms. In a study of child separation from family during armed conflict, Ressler et al.

(1988) note the underlying causes as including the conscription or imprisonment of parents, the abandonment of disabled children, the abduction of children by military forces and the expulsion of the child from the home for its own safety. But the authors conclude that poverty and single-parent status are the two family characteristics most commonly identified in unaccompanied children.

Social networks

> Hardship singles out your true friend (Khmer proverb, quoted by Mysliwiec, 1988:65).

Beyond the family are the ties between neighbours and friends, many of which are based on long-term residence in a local village or hamlet. Through local alliances families can obtain loans, share food, exchange labour, or collaborate in mutual protection — mechanisms that provide economic benefit and stave off destitution. Thus, the destruction of such ties due to forced relocation, collectivization and other strategies of war can powerfully undermine both family and individual resilience, as well as leading to the loss of essential survival and social skills.

The concept of "community" is widely employed in Cambodia today, especially with reference to an ideal that existed in the past and also to "community development" efforts in the present. However, there is often more ideology than fact in the usage of the term. Looking back to the time before the Pol Pot régime, people tend to recall traditional Cambodian villages as concrete, functioning communities that provided a supportive environment for all their members. In practice, however, rural villages were far from homogenous even before the outbreak of political violence and clear lines of tension have long existed. So, while it is certainly relevant when assessing resilience and vulnerability to identify the common interests and mutually supportive alliances that exist between people living in the same location, it would not be appropriate to romanticize these too much or to imply that they were inclusive or stable.

Cambodians, it seems, customarily relied far less on ties outside the family for social or economic support than many other rural societies. Although defined by a distinct territory and recognized as a separate administrative unit, the Cambodian village appears traditionally to have invoked little sense of community or collective solidarity. Anthropological research conducted in Cambodia in the 1960s, prior to the years of conflict, indicates that villages were minimally structured and embodied no single, typical pattern of interaction:

> . . . groups were formed for specific tasks but allowed to dissolve immediately thereafter. . . . The Cambodian villager emerges . . . as very much an individualist with a positive aversion to too much structuring of time or activities. In a situation where most Cambodian villagers were farmers engaged in rain-fed rice cultivation on small plots of land, there was no compelling reason for community organization above the level of the individual family (UNICEF, 1995:35).

Some villages had dispersed settlement patterns due to low population density and some were composed of a series of hamlets, both features serving to reduce village-wide co-operation. West Svay was found to have a low level of internal social differentiation, "no well-defined groups beyond the family and household, no clear-cut social stratification, and no rigid norms dictating interaction" (UNICEF, 1995:92). Indeed, the lack of indigenous, traditional, organized associations, clubs, factions, or other groups that are formed on non-kin principles is a striking feature of Cambodian village life (Ebihara, 1968). And attempts by the Khmer Rouge to structure and collectivize agricultural production and organize family life along communal lines were bitterly disliked by Cambodians.

That said, villagers were expected to like and help one another, and co-residents were perceived as trustworthy and good people — in contrast to "bad" strangers (Ebihara, 1968:174). Thus, co-operative work teams organized for agricultural labour and work parties formed for house construction or building communal wells might include friends and neighbours as well as kin. These would often prove a vital source of economic and social security:

> Our families had lived together for generations . . . there seemed to be nowhere else to go. And so there was a wide variety of *provas*, the loaning of belongings and labour. One family would exchange what they could spare for something else that they needed. I saw *provas* with chickens, ducks, cows, labour, buffalo, rice fields, sugar palms (Meas with Healy, 1995:20).

During the People's Republic of Kampuchea the *Krom Samaki* or "solidarity group", consisting of 10 to 15 families working with their own or communal paddy land, pooling labour, farm tools and animals and based on traditional mutual aid mechanisms, was introduced. Land distributed to the solidarity group was allotted on the basis of one or two hectares per family, depending on availability and quality. Drawing on research in Prey Veng province, Kiernan and Boua found that the *Krom* system provided an important safety net for the most vulnerable members of the village, ensuring that they were not forced to migrate to urban areas (cited in Mysliwiec, 1988:29). However, the system was not perceived positively in all quarters and was criticized by many international organizations and some Cambodians as an intermediary path to total socialist collectivization of agriculture (Mysliwiec, 1988; Ledgerwood, 1992).

> During the Vietnamese time we had shared land. It is better now we have our own land. At that time it wasn't good because when you did things together some depended on others. During the growing season there were few who worked on the land, but during the harvest there were many . . . (Farmers in Battambang District).

One source of dissent was the equal division of the harvest among group members, regardless of their labour contribution (Uimonen, 1994). Also, the groups were obliged to sell a proportion of their produce to the state at very low prices, thereby cutting profit. Economic liberalization in 1989 resulted in the dismantling of the co-operative *Krom Samaki* system and ending of subsidized prices for basic commodities.

Some observers (Uimonen, Kiernan, Mysliwiec) suggest that there has been a conscious attempt to return to pre-Khmer Rouge customs in a number of areas as a means of re-establishing social order. For example, labour exchange is still widely practised in Cambodia today within the extended family and between long-term neighbours. However, nowadays the labour must often be hired for cash — especially during rice cultivation. *Provas* sometimes take the form of share-cropping. Thus, Uimonen cites the case of Ream, a widow and her widowed daughter and her 3 children, who live together in Phum Srai, where they have 1.3 hectares of land. Because they lack labour, this land is all worked by other people on an exchange basis, in return for half the yield.

> People who don't have buffaloes or men to work can use *prova(s)*. *Prova(s)* is better than *Krom Samaki* — men with cattle plough, women transplant rice. *Prova(s)* — you help me and I help you. It's better (Uimonen, 1994:18).

The extent to which families and individuals can rely on such systems of mutual aid, particularly in areas where the greatest social upheavals and the largest concentrations of war-affected populations live, has still to be established.

While there are some data in Cambodia about changes in the structure and solidarity of villages in the last two and a half decades, there is hardly any information concerning the alliances made by children and youth based on their peer group. Yet, stability of the peer group during periods of political violence can be especially critical for older children, for whom family is but one reference point. In societies in conflict the peer group is sometimes perceived as the main source of vulnerability in children, since many children are recruited into armies or enticed by their peers into prostitution, substance abuse or other activities considered socially unacceptable. Hence the importance of social networks being built on positive role models if they are to be a source of resilience in children. On the other hand, it is also true that in some adverse situations, engaging in criminal activities or those considered anti-social is the most effective survival strategy for children and entails less risk than remaining within the family or at home.

The means of survival

Access to economic resources is fundamental to psycho-social resilience in both children and adults:

> Subsistence sufficiency is an important factor in family support of children. Destitute families that face great difficulties meeting subsistence needs may also have great difficulty providing nurturing care to their children. Some families feel forced to choose which children will survive the

realistic limitations of resources. Just as hungry children have difficulty concentrating on school tasks, the psycho-social well-being of a family is linked to its subsistence sufficiency. Without assistance, widows, widowers, abandoned spouses, spouses of missing persons and other single-headed households often have severe difficulty in surviving and providing for children (Ressler et al., 1992:182).

During periods of political violence, income and food supply are often threatened. Food shortages and famine have become a particular feature of internal conflict in many countries, largely because control of civilian populations is achieved either by removing them from their sources of livelihood altogether (through forced relocation, strategic hamleting, conscription or other tactics) or by destroying the resources upon which they depend. In most conflicts it is the poor who are most seriously affected, largely because their economic vulnerability prior to the outbreak of fighting undermines resilience during conflict. However, in the case of Cambodia during the Khmer Rouge time in particular, it was the rich and the urban dwellers who were the targets of violence and they who were rendered vulnerable and destitute.

There are several ways in which armed conflict undermines civilian economies, and the adverse impacts include: the destruction or confiscation of stored food and property, through military engagements, indiscriminate theft, looting or requisitioning; the reduction or cessation of food production through abandonment of land (due to forced migration, fear of military action or dissemination of landmines), or the destruction of crops or irrigation systems; and a shortage of labour for productive work, due to conscription, death, injury and other factors. The breakdown of agricultural extension and loss of valuable technical knowledge is a major problem in many conflict zones. The loss of livestock, due mainly to requisitioning or theft, can also have serious economic impacts, as can the obstruction of coping strategies by controls on movement (thereby stopping labour migration, trading, the collection of wild foods and similar survival strategies), bombing and other means. The interruption of commerce by preventing commercial food shipments, market operations or the sale of food in shops is common during conflict, as is a dramatic loss of income due to closure of factories, service establishments and other places of employment, withdrawal of private investment and conscription. Separation from food stocks, farm equipment, herds and income sources due to displacement or forced collectivization can also seriously undermine family welfare.

De Waal (1989) suggests that the obstruction of coping strategies is the most insidious and possibly the most important of these effects. Food security researchers have sought to establish the cycles by which people suffering from natural disasters repay debts, and rebuild reciprocal relationships and stocks after a famine. They have also sought, conversely, to identify the downward cycles whereby stocks are used, animals and other assets sold, reciprocal relationships are called upon or the household dispersed. Seasonal variation in food and income and variations in access at the community, household and individual levels can be considerable.

During periods of acute food insecurity, individuals and households typically sustain themselves by disposing of assets, particularly savings, disposable assets that were specifically acquired for such purposes (such as gold or livestock) and goods considered to be luxury items, like radios (Tickner 1996). In Cambodia, chickens and piglets are particularly important liquid assets. Another common response to food insecurity is to borrow food, or money to buy food, and in Cambodia these debts are usually incurred in the short, rather than long, term with relatives or friends (Tickner, 1996). In more extreme situations people will borrow rice or cash from a money lender, although this is normally a last resort because of the high rates of interest.

Economic diversification is an essential strategy of survival for many families. Diversification in the Cambodian context includes the labour exchange or share-cropping arrangements and the *Krom Samaki* system already mentioned. The out-migration from the community of individuals who then supply regular remittances to their families is another diversification strategy. In Cambodia, this includes remittances from the many people living overseas, although this income source was largely eliminated during the worst periods of fighting. Then there is the diversification of income sources obtained through the division of labour of family members across a broad range of occupations and activities. Talking about the economy of his family prior to the Vietnamese invasion, Meas Nee remarks:

> We had my father's money from the school teaching, and a rice field, and the animals, and the jobs my mother did. There was no idea of just one 'job'. Many small earnings added together made enough for the daily food. The word for the many things you do to get your rice and food is called '*rok si*' (Meas with Healy, 1995:21).

Aid interventions can also have a very significant impact on economic well-being in emergencies, and families often include the goods, services and other benefits distributed as part of relief packages in their overall economic planning. Nevertheless, as the work of researchers such as De Waal (1989) and Jackson (1987) shows, the impact of aid is not always positive. Families can be rendered more vulnerable by food aid, for example, because it can flood local markets and bring the prices of local produce down, or because it makes people dependent on food distributions.

Undoubtedly, economic stagnation, or economic decline, nationally in Cambodia is a major cause of impoverishment at the family and individual levels, as well as a potential source of psycho-social vulnerability in children. Cambodia's economy is founded on subsistence agriculture: even in 1992 only 13 per cent of the population was urban (Roberts and Williams, 1995). Access to rice land, and especially fertile land reliably supplied with water, is a key factor in economic well-being. However, land quality varies enormously within districts and communes, so economic differentiation at the local level can be quite marked. And food scarcity has a strong seasonal dimension, in that the proportion of households that go hungry steadily rises from May to August (reaching a peak between August and November) in most areas. Displacement, mines and other consequences of war have cut many families off from their lands.

During the Democratic Kampuchea period, the entire economic base of Cambodian society was completely reorganized as part of the overall strategy to become economically self-sufficient and at the same time maximize agricultural production: this was to have devastating economic impact. All forms of currency and trade were abolished and urban/industrial production was banned in favour of agriculture. The Khmer Rouge attempted to standardize agriculture and restore part of the water control systems of the ancient Khmer empire of Angkor. All urban dwellers other than the élite cadre of Khmer Rouge leaders were forced to abandon their homes and move to rural areas. Labour in agriculture was organized in the form of work teams rather than family or village groups, land tenure was revised and agriculture collectivized.

Between 1979 and 1982, under the rule of the People's Revolutionary Party, there was a consistent attempt to reconstruct the agricultural sector and regain self-sufficiency in food production, with a return to privatization and semi-socialist systems. The *Krom Samaki* was the key measure for improving production in fishing, agriculture and craft work. At this time, party members, peasants artisans and traders were in the main better off than people employed by the state — government officials, factory workers, professionals and the like. But economic recovery was severely hampered by ecological disasters and international isolation. For example, droughts and flooding in several parts of the country caused serious food losses and shortages, yet with international isolation emergency aid from Western nations was not forthcoming.

Economic liberalization and the influx of UNTAC and aid personnel in the early 1990s provided new economic opportunities for some Cambodians, particularly those living in urban areas. Yet, as noted, these benefits have largely been outweighed by the inflationary and distortionary effects on the economy, and by the corruption and exploitation associated with the recent social changes. It is widely thought that many Cambodians today are living in destitution far more severe than they were in the 1980s.

Leadership and moral authority

The existence of individuals, such as elders and religious or civic leaders, with special skills in problem solving and the capacity to give guidance and support can be an important source of resilience among children and adults. Effective leadership can contribute to building and maintaining moral and social codes, and reinforcing social consensus and social confidence. However, the potential for leaders to abuse their power may grow during political crises:

> In times of crisis, the government appointed village leader may be of help. Equally, he may be the one who interposes himself between the outside world and the villagers, exploiting them and inhibiting local initiative (Taylor, 1994:29).

It has already been mentioned that Cambodia is a hierarchical society — leadership being a significant factor in social interaction and social control. The country is ruled by an élite which, at one time, focused on the royal family and related aristocracy, high ranking officials in government and religious organizations, and a few very wealthy Cambodian or Sino-Cambodian business people and professionals (Ebihara, 1968). In the words of a Cambodian man working for an NGO:

> I have learnt by war and régime . . . now all we want is stability. I understand that people believe Sihanouk was not democratic and that he headed a hierarchical monarchy seeing himself as the 'father of his children'. But he was a good ruler, he was a traditional king and there was no war here then because people followed him.

As we have seen, the bulk of the population has always been made up of the rural peasantry, fisher people and crafts people. But unskilled urban labourers constitute a growing proportion of the population as the towns and cities expand. Middle-income groups, such as the business community, professionals, middle or low ranking government officials and office workers, comprise but a small percentage, their numbers having been much reduced by the Khmer Rouge atrocities.

In the 1960s there existed several layers of authority in rural areas: the provincial governors, district chiefs, sub-district chiefs and finally, the village headmen (Ebihara, 1968). All but the latter two posts were filled by the appointment of the Ministry of the Interior from the ranks of civil servants. Tradition and patronage are important principles governing relationships between the élite and the mass of the population in Cambodia, and the more powerful families in a village would provide economic security and protection for the weaker ones, in return for their loyalty (Harmer, 1995). Yet, there is no evidence that the patron-client system was ever formalized and, according to Ebihara, leadership, planning and organization have never been strong in Cambodia, lay positions associated with the temples offering the only avenue for community participation and leadership outside the family.

Community leadership, insofar as it existed, was provided in part by the prominent families of the village, and was an extension of the authority of these families, who were usually related to each other and to other families in the area. Thus even in the public sphere the family was an essential structure.

The other sources of community leadership were the monks and the *achar* [lay elders of Buddhist temples], both of whom drew their authority from their standing as religious figures, once again immediately related to the religious observances of individual families, but also having an autonomous status as members of the monastic establishment, and deriving prestige from their superior knowledge (UNICEF, 1995:33).

Buddhist monks and nuns have customarily provided extensive pastoral care in the form of shelter and food and other services throughout Cambodia. Monks would frequently mediate in land disputes and mobilize people to build roads or other community projects, as well as providing education for children. The *kruu Khmer*, or traditional healers, are another source of authority at the local level and have long provided moral and spiritual guidance, as well as health care. The word *"kruu"*. . . means a patient person, a respected person, a person who teaches knowledge and arts to his disciples" (IRC, 1990:1). There are many kinds of *kruu* and they fulfil a broad range of important social and health functions. There are the healers — the herbalists, the medics, and the doctors. The *kruu pleeng* are the music teachers. The *kruu bangrien* are the school teachers and the monks are the *kruu oppacia* (IRC, 1990:1). In the past the *kruu* were respected as people of wisdom, they were wise in the ways of living and ethics.

The more recent system of party-appointed groups and village leaders, first founded during the PKR period, remains important today at the local level. In many cases continuity of these leaders has been maintained even with displacement, because people would often flee with their leaders. Whatever the strengths of individual leaders, national or local, some Cambodians express an ambivalence about their role, as a returnee from the United States suggests:

> We have leaders now: there is the King and the government. They represent a symbol that people could look up to, that people should be looking up to. But they don't. We don't have any aspirations. . . . There are respected elders in every community, but few people are willing to replace them because they fear that gaining the respect of the local community will be seen as a threat to the government or Khmer Rouge.

This is another legacy of the Khmer Rouge rule. Since people in positions of responsibility — school teachers, monks and village leaders, for example were often the first to be targeted by the Khmer Rouge, many are now unwilling to take an active civic role since they fear the consequences should the Khmer Rouge return.

2.3

The Efficacy of Cultural Constructs

Giving meaning to violence and suffering

Eisenbruch (1991a) and Metraux (undated) make a powerful case in their research for continuity of beliefs, attitudes and values as being central to psycho-social resilience. Although they imply a rather static, homogenous view of culture, this thesis is consistent with our point, made earlier, that individuals understand stressful experiences by referring to a core of cultural constructs, norms and values and it is these that underpin healing and recovery. Buddhism is a central force in Cambodia and while many things have been lost or greatly changed due to the conflict, the features of the past that remain are of great importance to people, as one middle aged man explained: "Although there have been many changes in government we survive, this must be because Buddhism remains" (Khmer man working for an International Agency). Many Buddhist traditions have been maintained, as noted by an expatriate NGO worker "although the level of understanding of Buddhism is low as the people with the knowledge are not there, Cambodians are still deeply Buddhist". He thought if a model for peace existed it would be within the Buddhist teachings. Certainly the importance of an integral focus on both the individual and the collective is eloquently expressed in the following statement that was written on a series of banners carried at the recent Dhammayietra (peace walk):

The Suffering of Cambodia has been Deep
From Deep Suffering comes Compassion
Great Compassion makes a Heart of Peace
A Peaceful Heart makes a Peaceful Person
A Peaceful Person makes a Peaceful Family
A Peaceful Family makes a Peaceful Community
A Peaceful Community makes a Peaceful Nation
A Peaceful Nation makes a Peaceful World

There is much discussion — some of it highly politicized — in Cambodia today about "traditional Khmer culture". Some of this discussion focuses on the role Cambodian culture supposedly plays in impeding economic and social development and obstructing social healing. Thus, for example, expatriate aid workers sometimes ascribe the social and economic difficulties faced by Cambodians at the present time to cultural conditioning, which they suggest induces fatalism in the face of adversity. Buddhists, they note, believe that once their karma is "spoilt" by participation — willing or otherwise — in violent or other damaging events, their fate will forever remain bad.

But the issue of whether or not Cambodian culture acts as a straightjacket is a complex one because, as mentioned, even though culture encapsulates the past in some way, it is not fixed; nor does it make up a coherent, systematic whole:

> The qualities associated with shifting cultural values, the dynamics in the articulation of group identity, are the premises upon which allocation of social accountability is negotiated. These things are the subject of dissent, and are inevitably more elusive at times of stress than they are in periods of relative political and economic stability (Allen, 1989:48).

Allen warns not to conflate ideology with reality: ideology may be like a cultural straightjacket, but this is likely to be very different from the reality of social change: "society . . . is always in a state of flux, for it is continuously being constructed" (p.50). The ideology of continuity with the past, with past beliefs and values may, as Eisenbruch and Metraux argue, be essential to psycho-social healing and it may also act, as some expatriates suggest, as a conservative force impeding change and development. However, cognitive structures and processes are really quite fluid. Indeed, some expatriates in Cambodia are more concerned to highlight what they see to be the cynical manipulation of Buddhist tradition and beliefs rather than the efficacy of Buddhist beliefs. They cite cases in which young men are said sometimes to join the monkshood simply in order to collect enough money to enable them to marry (international NGO worker). They also argue that while pagodas are being rebuilt in large numbers, this is for ceremonial rather than educational and spiritual ends. One observer commented on the weak formal belief system in Cambodia, arguing that the monks do not play an active spiritual role (international NGO worker).

Whatever the meaning given to violence, illness and suffering in Cambodia, an assessment of vulnerability and resilience in children needs to take into account those norms, values and practices which reinforce, and those which potentially undermine, individual coping capacity. Certainly an analysis of psycho-social vulnerability in children and adults should take account of any beliefs that could be contributory. Cambodian attitudes towards amputees have been cited as one example of how fundamental Buddhist precepts can be a potential source of psycho-social susceptibility:

> Wholeness of body is a key concept in the world-view of Buddhists. Buddhists also believe strongly in the concept of karma, which is a belief that how past lives are lived determines the present, and the outcome of the next life hinges on behaviour in this one. These two different tenets of Buddhism shape the opposing forces that interact to determine the acceptance of amputees of their condition. On the one hand, they accept their disability as part of their karma, which explains their often stoic attitudes in dealing with their condition, but on the other hand, they cannot come to terms with the rejection of themselves and from their community that they have lost part of their bodies, thus destroying their 'wholeness' (Foong, 1995:6).

Heng Foong maintains that because they are no longer "whole", amputees in Cambodia are heavily stigmatized. They "often find themselves shunned by all strata of society, whether they be farmers, monks and even family and relatives" (1995:6).

2.4

Access to Services

Access to shelter, safe areas for play and recreation and places for storing food and personal possessions securely can be critical to psycho-social welfare. Information is another crucial resource during adversity, since both adults and children need to make informed decisions and judgements which may be fundamental to their safety. By the same token, misinformation and propaganda can render civilians extremely vulnerable. However, access to basic services (education, health, transport, water and sanitation) is possibly especially important for children, since these affect not only psycho-social well-being but also survival itself.

Services have symbolic value in the context of conflict because they represent political and administrative control, as well as indicating normality and continuity in social processes: doing normal things helps create structure out of chaos. With the exception of health care for the aged, children, and especially infants and young children, are often more dependent than adults on basic services. While all services can enhance the quality of life for children generally, some — health, water and sanitation in particular — are essential for their survival.

There is very little information about the coverage of services in Cambodia in the past, but the indications are that until the 1980s very few people had access to even basic services. For example, the education and health systems were almost entirely destroyed during the 1970s. Surveys show a gradual improvement in coverage and quality of services, however, over the last two decades. For example, national sanitation coverage, an underlying determinant of child survival, although still very low with only 16 per cent of households nationally having access, has improved since 1990 — when the rate was 6 per cent. Coverage of safe drinking water is also low in comparison to other countries in the region, with only 36 per cent of households having access in the 1990 to 1995 period. With both water and sanitation there is a very marked discrepancy between rural and urban provision, and Phnom Penh has significantly better services than all other areas. Thus, while 84 per cent of the population of Phnom Penh has access to sanitation facilities, other urban areas have a coverage of 37 per cent and rural areas only 6 per cent (UNICEF, 1995).

Formal health provision has yet to be re-established in many parts of the country. Nevertheless, where public services are running efficiently and cheaply they are reportedly well used. National BCG (tuberculosis vaccine) coverage reached 78 per cent in 1994, for example. There remain, however, many problems in terms of support for health care (UNICEF, 1995). Essential drugs are in extremely short supply, for example, and when aid from the former Eastern bloc dried up in the late 1980s, the government was unable to provide even the most basic drugs and medical materials. In the early 1990s, NGOs and bilateral agencies were the only source — and since more than 50 per cent of the national drug budget comprised of loans that did not extend beyond 1995, Cambodia will need to find other grant or loan assistance in the foreseeable future. Because of the many shortcomings, Cambodians have little confidence in formal health provision. Self treatment and traditional medicine are used far more frequently and the *kruu Khmer* remain the most important providers of health care and advice.

Monks traditionally played an important role as teachers in the temple schools, but few monks today are sufficiently literate to teach. By the end of 1979 all state schools had been abandoned and less than 5,000 teachers remained, the majority having died or left the country (UNICEF, 1990). Impressive efforts were made throughout the 1980s to rebuild the system, but much work still has to be done. Drop-out rates are high, and of those who enrolled in first grade in 1989 only 34 per cent had remained in school up to grade five. Children stay away from school for a number of reasons. Many must help their families earn a living, others may be too malnourished or cannot afford the enrolment fees. And the continuing conflict in some areas seriously affects access, especially for displaced families. Because of the destruction of schools and the high proportion of children in the population, classes are at present very overcrowded — especially in urban areas — even with the poor attendance rates.

Low wages have made it impossible to attract more people into the teaching profession — and low salaries invite corruption. In both rural and urban areas, and even at university level, payments are commonly made to teachers for certification (personal communication, Uimonen). A community development worker in a village in Banan district explained the problem:

> Teachers in the past are not like teachers in the present. Not only is their salary low but they are not well trained and have to be forced to do anything good . . . they only focus on the money and they have to give extra classes to survive. . . .

In the cities UNICEF aims to fulfil teachers' needs so that they don't have to find extra work and so they can devote themselves to their one job better. It forces them to work regularly. Here the classes are often cancelled — there is really no control over teachers. I worry so much about this. How can I have any success in community development work if no-one goes to school? (Cambodian community development worker).

A woman from the same community commented:

The teachers are often absent, just one small ceremony and they shut the school. On the other hand from our side we sometimes don't allow the children to attend school . . . with the floods, for instance, we need them to help us with the work and with the security situation sometimes we are just worried about their safety so we keep them at home (A women in a Banan District village).

Other women present on the occasion showed that they agreed fully with what she was saying.

2.5

The Attributes and Disposition of the Individual Child

We have argued that people, including children, display both resilience and vulnerability in the face of adversity. As mentioned, children are not mere recipients of experience; nor are they passive. Children have strengths and susceptibilities which in themselves contribute to coping in times of adversity. Regardless of a child's experience of conflict, or his or her social, family or economic circumstances, individual children vary enormously in their capacity to process and cope with stressful events. Thus, assessment of vulnerability in children needs to take into consideration not just the structural factors that mediate the experience of violence, but also the capacities and weaknesses of the individual child. Unfortunately, there is very little information about children in Cambodia since there has been virtually no systematic research on the subject. So, in order to build up a picture of the possible range of individual factors affecting psycho-social resilience in children, we have had to draw on research from other areas. The factors that have been found determinant elsewhere are described below.

Social status

Information derived for vulnerability assessments of Cambodian children needs to be properly disaggregated to expose gender, caste, class, ethnicity and age differences, as well as rural or urban abode. This is because, as noted earlier, differentiation within childhood based on distinctions of social status fundamentally affects the psycho-social well-being of children. This is for two reasons.

I) Because of the social and economic roles assigned to different categories of children and the different value awarded these categories of children, exposure to violence is not equally distributed in the child population:

> . . . vulnerability is not simply a matter of accident or chance. . . . Seldom are all children equally esteemed by adults: a child's age, physical attributes, personality, sex or birth order may crucially influence its status and welfare within the family and in society as a whole. Frequently family or household survival is secured by exposing one or more children to greater danger: the children so exposed may be the ones most expendable or those with the greatest earning potential (Boyden, 1994:264).

Thus, for example, in societies in which boys achieve the social status of manhood by taking up arms they face particular risk of exposure to violence during armed conflict. In a study of Somalia, Jama (1992) notes how, as tribal warriors and looters, school-age boys became crucial to family survival and defence during the conflict. By contrast, in the Shan state in Burma girls have borne the greater economic and social burden and face the greatest physical and psycho-social risks. Families are able to protect boys from enlistment by sending them at age 12 or so to a monastery. Girls, on the other hand, remain in their village and hence are required by the military to undertake duty labour, which is onerous and sometimes dangerous, or are sold into prostitution in Thailand, providing one of the few sources of income in this impoverished area of Burma.

II) There is also the possibility that children in different categories may be genetically, or through their socialization, predisposed to respond in different ways to adversity, either increasing their coping capacity or rendering them more susceptible. Research in this area is not well developed though and the evidence is far from conclusive (Cairns, 1996). For instance, some studies note differences between girls and boys with respect to their reactions and state of mind in the context of organized violence, although there is no clear theory as to whether this is due to gender socialization or innate distinctions. Cairns notes that the general literature on childhood tends to agree that at least up to the age of puberty boys are more likely to be at risk than girls when exposed to a range of stressors. According to Punamaki (1989) this has also been the general pattern in studies focusing specifically on the impact of political violence. McCallin and Fozzard (1991), for example, reported boys as being more nervous and fearful in the presence of strangers and more often expressing a need than girls to talk about their experience of distressing or unpleasant events. However, they found girls to be more fearful of the dark, more often seeking approval, affection and reassurance and more likely to express a sense of hopelessness about the future.

Whether such differences are innate or socially constructed, that they exist demonstrates the importance of not lumping children together as a homogenous and "vulnerable" group, but of seeing them in all their individual diversity.

Clearly, age provides one of the most important dimensions of differentiation within childhood. And it is logical to assume that at some points in their lives children can be more vulnerable to psycho-social distress than at others. But the research yields little information on this topic. Cairns (1996) notes that this is partly because most studies are based on relatively small samples or are confined to one or two age levels only.

In so far as knowledge or understanding of events helps children to frame their experience and thereby to process and cope with it, older children who tend to be better informed and cognitively more developed than younger ones may be somewhat protected. However, each developmental age has its own vulnerabilities and ways of exhibiting distress. For example, Leyens and Mahjoub (undated) note that children between 2 and 5 years of age and adolescents are consistently found in research to be the most susceptible to war trauma. As far as these authors are concerned, the significance of these life phases is that they constitute the periods when children are most influenced by others. Young children's reactions, for example, closely reflect the responses of those caring for them. By contrast, research with school children in war-time England (Dunsdon, 1941, cited in Cairns, 1996) established that stress was at its lowest in the 2-5 years age group, while psychological symptoms predominated among 5-7 year olds and psychosomatic illnesses became more common between 11 and 14.

Personality and coping style

Some children are by disposition or temperament better able to manage stress than others; this is a matter of their personality structure and coping style (Ressler et al., 1992). Exposure to a hazardous event renders people vulnerable and each individual reacts in his or her own way. Psychologists have found that while in a vulnerable state, the individual may experience an initial rise in tension and respond with one or more problem-solving measures. If this activity does not succeed, tension will peak and with it feelings of depression, helplessness, and hopelessness will usually appear (Bromley, 1987:237).

It has been suggested that children who actively try to assume some control over their lives while remaining hopeful about the future and who are flexible, adaptable and possess problem-solving skills, are less vulnerable than those who passively accept their condition (Punamaki, 1987). The processing of feelings is partially defined by culture, in that different cultures articulate grief, anger and fear in different ways. Children must find adaptive ways of dealing with stressful experiences and associated emotions if they are to cope in adversity. Constructive coping techniques help children manage their feelings and reactions, while destructive or passive ones tend to accentuate difficulties. However, Cairns comments that theories of this kind are still speculative because studies measuring the child's pre-morbid personality are lacking. He notes the work conducted in Israel by Miligram and Miligram (1976) as being the most thorough in this regard, in that it began prior to the outbreak of war and continued during actual conflict. The authors found a tendency among children with low peacetime anxiety scores to have high war-time anxiety scores and vice versa. Their explanation was that low peacetime scores represented a personality factor, or trait anxiety, as opposed to state anxiety, concluding, in other words, that the temperamentally anxious child responds to war with less anxiety.

The need to call on inner resources for survival was acute during the Khmer Rouge era, a time characterized by total control of practically all aspects of civilian life by the militarized state. Adaptability and possession of problem-solving skills were important contributors to survival. Cambodia has seen a succession of authoritarian régimes and people have had to adjust constantly what they do and say to suit the political climate of the time simply to stay alive. Thus, as one aid worker commented: "Cambodians have been forced to become chameleons". Similarly, a Buddhist nun noted that:

> Even before the Vietnamese régime and the Pol Pot régime, there was the French régime and the Thai régime . . . all these people come in and out trying to take control, fighting each other to get power. And it's amazing — they all expect us to change to adapt to their ways of living! . . . . Sometimes it's difficult for people to know what to think anymore (Nun, 60 years old, from village in Province of Battambang).

To keep a low profile by feigning ignorance was of critical importance to survival:

> There is a Cambodian saying learned in Pol Pot times: 'plant the Kapok tree'. It is a play on the words, *'dem kor'*. The allusion is to deaf mute. The meaning is that you will get further if you pretend to know nothing, hear nothing, say nothing (Meas with Healy, 1995:30).

This was an important protective strategy:

> Fear, violence, and the frequent human rights violations that occur in the Khmer camps have reinforced the *tiing moong* — or 'dummy personality' forged during the 1975-1979 genocidal period in Cambodia. *Tiing moong* is a Cambodian term used by the Khmer to describe their behaviour under the Khmer Rouge. Many individuals, in order to survive, had to act as if they were deaf, dumb, foolish, confused, and stupid.

The Khmer learned to obey orders without asking questions or complaining. If they appeared to be 'smart', they knew they would be tortured or executed (Mollica et al., undated:96).

Yet the imperative of survival also forced adults and children to break social norms or taboos or to disregard the rules of the military. To be able to lie, scavenge, steal and hide food and other goods, for example, was essential. May Someth writes: "The revolution forced me to become a liar, a thief, a smuggler, a classical dancer, a refugee and finally a stateless person" (1986 cited in Ledgerwood et al., 1994:21). These were often high risk strategies:

We all ate together, but sometimes when people were hungry they stole fruits and vegetables. When the team leader saw this he reprimanded the person who had stolen once or twice. Then the person was beaten or killed (Ream, a 60-year-old widow cited in Uimonen, 1994:8).

Humour is another capacity identified through research as being vital to resilience and coping (Vanistendael, 1995). During the course of the field work for this study it was observed that people quite often used laughter and humour when recounting a particularly difficult or serious experience or feeling. Thus, the village leader in Phum Somnagn, when speaking of the problems of food in the village, commented on the irony of the situation: "each day some people wake up hungry and all they can find around them are things you can't eat". He then burst out laughing and continued to laugh and laugh. When asked how he found the capacity for such laughter he replied: "well we can either laugh or we can cry . . . it is better to laugh". To understand what role humour plays in peoples' lives and its possible use as a coping strategy would require much more research, though.

Hope is another resource essential to resilience during adversity. Many Cambodians, however, have found it impossible to sustain hope during the 25 long years of violence. In the words of one Khmer woman:

> I have a cloth hanging up in my home that says, 'to live is to hope'. I look at that every morning. Sometimes I want to tear it down and wrap it round my neck. But I know I must have hope for the sake of my children (cited in Mysliwiec, 1988:56-7).

The Buddhist understanding of karma most likely influences attitudes in relation to hope because of the sense of fatalism it can generate. Several Khmer mentioned their feeling that their karma weighs heavily on them. Some mentioned that they lived in dread that the violence would all begin again.

Cognitive competence

Cognitive competence is an important mediating factor in resilience and vulnerability. Children of at least average intelligence can enhance their own coping because intelligence means the ability to solve problems by identifying alternatives and thinking up creative solutions. Critical thinking also: "helps shield the child from simplistic interpretations of experience that are self-defeating and socially destructive in the long run" (Gabarino et al., 1991). Gabarino (1991) suggests that cognitive competence may be adversely affected by exposure to stressful events, such that repeated exposure presents a cumulative risk, shown in a decline in Intelligence Quota (IQ) in pre-school children.

Physical health

Research shows that psycho-social welfare is aggravated by poor physical condition due to inadequate nutrition and/or ill health. Cambodia's rural population is today among the poorest in the world and widespread poverty and the limitations of the health service render children and women, in particular, vulnerable to a range of health problems and premature death.

> The morbidity and mortality indicators reflect more than two decades of inadequate diet, poor water and sanitation and low quality medical care, exacerbated by civil war and landmines (UNICEF, 1995:18).

The very poor state of physical health among Cambodian children no doubt also has implications for psycho-social welfare. Infant mortality is 115 per 1,000 live births, the highest in the region, the average IMR for East Asia and the Pacific being 42. Under 5 mortality runs at 181 per 1,000, as compared to 56 for the region as a whole. Life expectancy at birth is below 50 years, while regionally it is 62.6. Maternal mortality is one of the highest in the world.

Even before birth, poor maternal nutrition contributes to low birth-weight and other problems. One Khmer woman noted that the severe under-nourishment suffered by her mother while pregnant with her younger brother during the Pol Pot time had lasting repercussions:

> I was always worried about my mother [during the Khmer Rouge Régime] who had to work really hard even when she was pregnant and she didn't have enough food for my brother when he was born. Now I can see the effect on him. He's not as smart as the rest of us — he's more slow — not so clever (Khmer woman working for an international NGO).

The illnesses and nutritional problems affecting children vary from one region to another and between urban and rural areas. Infant mortality in Cambodia is largely due to prematurity or low birth-weight and delivery complications. Under-nourishment is a chronic problem among children and an important contributor to high infant/child morbidity and mortality. Protein-energy malnutrition is the most common nutritional problem. A nutrition survey of 427 children aged 13 to 36 months in Kampong Speu province indicated that 53 per cent were less than 80 per cent of their normal height (UNICEF, 1995:48).

Acute respiratory infections, followed by diarrhoeal diseases and malaria, are the major cause of mortality in the 1 to 4 age group. Acute respiratory infections in children account for 52 per cent of medical consultations, and diarrhoeal diseases, 21 per cent. Dengue haemorrhagic fever, once a problem among urban children only, now occurs in rural areas also. Measles and tuberculosis are also common among Cambodian children. Vitamin A and iodine deficiency and the widespread prevalence of schistosomiasis in areas along the Mekong river are particularly significant in terms of morbidity, if not mortality, in children.

PART 3

The Psycho-Social Impacts of Conflict

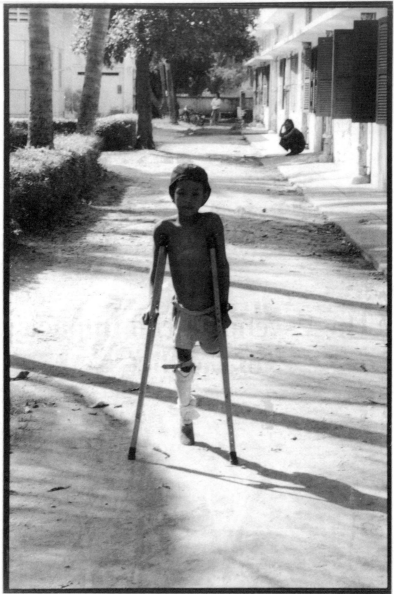

Boy at Wat Than rehabilitation centre in Phnom Penh.
Credit: Peter Williams/WCC Photo.

3.1

Impacts on Family

Separation and loss

In Cambodia, the integrity of the family has been consistently under attack in recent years, not just because of political violence but also due to rapid economic and social change. This presents a direct threat to children's resilience. During the consultative process on the psycho-social consequences of conflict in Cambodia which formed part of the UNRISD research programme on The Challenge of Rebuilding War-torn Societies and involved more than 300 Cambodians and expatriates, it was concluded that:

> . . . certain social relations and institutions which previously gave meaning and support to people's lives have weakened. The extended family networks and patron-client relations

which formed the basis of local support systems have experienced considerable upheaval, resulting in a society [where there is less ability and commitment to care for those who are less well off] (Harmer, 1995:14).

A large number of people were killed or forcibly separated during the Khmer Rouge era. Arranged (or, rather, forced) marriages were common and many of those so united were subsequently separated and divorced.

Before Pol Pot it wasn't like it is now, families were together then. Now people just divorce; maybe they had been forced to marry someone and then after 1979 they just split up and the children suffered a lot because of that (Khmer woman working for an international NGO).

Many people lost all their personal documents and mementoes at this time, and some changed their names and cut themselves off from relatives overseas in order to hide their foreign connections from the authorities. This made communications between separated relatives very difficult. After the downfall of Pol Pot, large numbers of Cambodians fled the country, a percentage to remain abroad indefinitely. Some were subsequently reunited, but many remained permanently cut off from each other. Continued international isolation after the departure of the Khmer Rouge, combined with the total breakdown of communications, further impeded reunification.

The following account highlights a number of the problems people faced.

Khmer NGO worker:
"A relative of mine, a woman, was married to a soldier during the Pol Pot time; she went with him because of the situation. Then in 1979 the Vietnamese came so that people were able to go back to their families. This relative looked for her family and found them.

"Her husband was not educated, so it was difficult for her to stay with him. He beat her and did not treat her well. Her mother wasn't happy with the man because he came from a different [social] level; it was difficult for the family to accept him. Finally, they divorced. Now he is very poor and a "cyclo" driver. He plays cards and drinks a lot.

"They had a child together and now she is married to another man, with whom she has three children; her son from her first marriage lives with them too. He used to be a good child for his mother and his second father but now he is 13 and his mother always complains that he doesn't go to school and that he sleeps in other families' homes. He is affected by seeing the difference between his father and his mother. His mother is worried about him seeing his father because of the company he keeps. It's not that she doesn't want him to see his father, only she wants him to be educated well before he does so that he can make a good decision when the time comes.

"This woman, my relative, has a heart problem. When she is angry with her son she can get easily shocked. She beats him now because she can no longer go in a good way with him.

"His step father was good to him at first, but now he is growing up to be bad. As the man is not his real father he can't do what he wants to him; he doesn't have the authority, and so he can't make sure he grows up to be better. So now they are not close any longer and there is jealousy between the children. All this is causing the family many problems."

Collectivization and the division of the labour force into work gangs was a conscious strategy used by the military to control civilian labour and civilian activity. This isolated children from their families:

> Children were often separated from parents, and adolescents were usually grouped in mobile working units located at some distance from their families. As children were physically separated from parents, parents ceased to have authority over them. Husbands and wives could also be separated from one another. The extended family, and in many cases even the nuclear family as an economic and residential unit, ceased to exist, as did its ability to control, support and comfort its members (Ledgerwood, et al., 1994:13).

It was intended that Angkar, the political unit of the Khmer Rouge, would replace the family as the prime social unit. Sain (a 28 year-old woman) recalls her childhood and how she felt about the way Angkar ruled her life:

> During Pol Pot I lived with the team leader, not with my family . . . When we did something wrong we were beaten. In the meetings they also told all the children not to miss their families because Angkar would take care of them, not their parents or their brothers and sisters. But sometimes I ran home because I missed my family. And then the teacher beat me. But I always said I liked Angkar. Everybody said they liked it, but in our thoughts we didn't like Angkar. The children were very important to Angkar because they worked very hard (Uimonen, 1994:7).

Today, economic liberalization and destitution are further attacking family strength and durability. The situation of one woman in Banan district exemplifies this:

My husband was getting desperate for work, so he asked me
to sell my land so that I could give him the money to go to
Sisophon to start up a business. I sold my land for him, gave
the pieces of gold to him . . . then he left me for another woman.
Now I am left alone and have no land.

While there are no reliable statistics on the numbers of children without
family support, the risk of family separation appears to have grown in
contemporary Cambodia with high rates of rural to urban migration,
since a significant proportion of migrants, including children, travel to
the city alone. In the countryside there is a serious lack of economic
opportunity, exaggerated by poor security due to banditry, political
violence and landmines, and environmental degradation. During the
UNTAC period especially, but also since then, towns have appeared to
offer better employment and higher incomes.

Some families opt to deliver one or more of their children into the care
of city-dwellers as one means of reducing family subsistence
requirements. This practice can provide children with new
opportunities, especially as education services expand in urban areas,
and certainly helps their transition into urban life. But it can present
a risk because, apart from cutting children off from their families, it
sometimes involves a payment, which in the modern context makes
children highly susceptible to traffickers. Whether sold into domestic
service or prostitution, the commoditization of children is apparently
a growing problem.

One woman whose husband died sent her children away from
her because she couldn't support them alone. She sent her
eldest child to the monks and the second one to the Khmer
Rouge area to look after the cattle because in that way they
would both have food. The girls she kept with her, although
one is now sold (International NGO expatriate worker).

The difficulty families face trying to provide for children in situations of economic and political insecurity is expressed by an expatriate development worker:

> When we are talking about children the family is so important because along with the community they live in it provides a first safety net, something that the government and NGOs can never replace. When the family breaks down the impact is huge. This breakdown causes a feeling of a loss of control over one's life and to recover this is so important. But if you are fighting for your survival you can't support your children properly and so the situation is perpetuated. People live with a fear that there will be a repeat of events and this effects their confidence and thus their ability to regain control over their lives (International Agency worker).

Intra-familial violence

Separation, loss and destitution all threaten the quality of intra-familial relations, rendering children vulnerable to domestic violence and other forms of abuse. The destruction of the authority structure within the family due to trauma in adults or other problems has been cited as one cause because it undermines family solidarity and adult authority especially. Elders find they cannot gain the respect or confidence of the young.

> The Pol Pot time made me very sad as I saw families fighting each other, fathers and sons scolding each other — it was such a difficult time because I had never seen anything like it before. It was especially difficult because in Cambodia it is our culture to respect the elderly whatever they do, even

if you know they are wrong . . . (Khmer woman working in an international NGO).

Indeed, the level of day-to-day violence within and outside the family in Cambodia is a major concern of many aid workers at the present time and has become an important topic for both research and intervention.

> The level of violence, exacerbated by the customary availability of weapons, prevailing for some 25 years, has left its marks on Khmer society. The further one moves away from major population centres, the more difficult it is to rely on 'law and order', and the more there is room for violent . . . exercise of illegitimate power. . . . Typically road tolls, protection money and 'rent' have to be paid by people living or moving about in the countryside. A large number of Cambodian men have, in one way or the other, been active in the war. Violence is easily resorted to, and many conflicts that start as trivial squabbles finish on a violent note. Violence is also domesticated in the sense that weapons are sold in the markets and mines are used to seal off private property. Furthermore, soldiers, or former soldiers, knowing no other way of living and having no means to sustain themselves, are quick to turn to banditry or to other extortionary activities (Ovesen, et al., 1995:28).

Social psychologist Seanglim Bit accounts for the pervasiveness of violence in Cambodian society by proposing the notion of a "warrior heritage" (1990). Teachers even fear for their safety in school, as one male teacher explained:

> It is difficult for me to keep control, especially as teachers are not able to use physical force anymore. In the past teachers always used physical punishment. . . . But if I hurt a child

now I could be in trouble especially if there are soldiers' children there. They can bring guns into school or they might come to my home and just shoot me (Teacher in a village in Battambang Province).

The first study on domestic violence in Cambodia was carried out by the Project Against Domestic Violence (PADV) in 1994. And in 1995 a statistical study on the prevalence of, and practices and attitudes in relation to, domestic violence was conducted by the Secretariat of State for Women's Affairs together with PADV, for use in programme planning and research. A conference in December 1994, "Wife Abuse in the Family: Violating the Rights of Women in Cambodia", led to the Cambodian National Declaration and Plan of Action Against Domestic Violence.

The intensity of violence perpetrated against women was found by the study to be extremely severe. Some see the problem as being directly attributable to behaviours learned through participation in armed conflict. As wife-battering is considered an internal family matter by the courts, police and local authorities, abusers go unpunished, while victims are merely encouraged to be patient. Mechanisms for conflict resolution are limited and, although partly due to the increase in poverty and political and social unrest, "sexism, culture, social mores and traditional public attitudes cause and perpetuate domestic violence" (Zimmerman, 1994).

Alcohol abuse is the most frequently cited correlate of domestic violence. Reported increases in the extent of domestic violence are, however, attributed by Cathy Zimmerman to experiences during the Khmer Rouge régime and to the decades of violent war to which Cambodians have been exposed. With the Khmer Rouge atrocities, families have been hard pressed to remain united: "In face of this revolution, the strategy for survival was to keep one's own council and to assume that all around were potential enemies" (Taylor, 1994:28). Value changes of this sort have serious emotional consequences:

> . . . now people are too poor to help one another, but its not just that they are poor: it depends on their heart, too. Some people are good and some are bad. My grandmother takes care of my nieces and nephews. She has a good heart. But my father's family, they are very poor and they don't take care of extra people. You see, the Pol Pot time taught us to feed ourselves before others, even if they were our mothers and fathers. So now we are a bit cut off from each other emotionally (Khmer woman working in an international NGO).

It is not known what effects this kind of emotional withdrawal might have on children, although it could be perceived as a form of neglect which often has long-term psycho-social consequences. These assertions about the poor quality of family life in Cambodia are quite common among expatriates and Khmer who work in the aid community. Whether or not they are valid merits proper investigation.

Demographic distortion

Another lasting effect of conflict, and especially of the Khmer Rouge rule, has been a major change in the demographic structure of Cambodian society. Among the many who have died, men predominate. There now exists in Cambodia a disproportionate number of adult females to males; of the present population over 18, around 55 to 65 per cent are female (UNICEF, 1995).

> The widows come in two sorts: the so-called Pol Pot widows, who lost their husbands during the atrocities of 1975-1979, and the new widows, who lost their husbands more recently.

These later deaths are often the result of military action or are caused by land mine explosions. Both fighting soldiers and civilians are affected in this way (Taylor, 1994:12).

Demographic distortion is exacerbated by widespread wife abandonment; the term "widow" applies also to those women abandoned by their husbands:

> Women complain of increasing problems of marital infidelity from their husbands caused by the disproportionate ratio of women to men and the high number of widows. Relationships have changed and families are no longer intact and supportive (Mysliwiec, 1988:11).

One consequence of the present demographic structure is said to be the high incidence of female headed households in Cambodia today. Some 20 per cent of households are headed by women (UNICEF, 1995:30). The process of granting asylum to refugees throughout the 1980s and early 1990s and the more recent repatriations from the Thai border camps contributed further to female headship and female management of households. Widows without access to male labour are held to be among the poorest of the poor: "Of the new widows, those with many young children are especially badly off" (Taylor, 1994:12). Although widowhood obviously has implications for women beyond the economic:

> There are many women in this community like me — without any husband. We all have difficulties, we miss our husbands, we miss the family discussion, we have difficult feelings. But those women who have cows and land and adult children are better off than those without. For them perhaps they are even better off without their husbands (Single woman in Phum Somnagn).

A woman who lost her husband during the Khmer Rouge period refers to the loneliness:

> I just feel a deep sadness and very much alone. . . . When I get up in the morning I feel very heavy, like something pressing on my shoulders. But I cannot talk to anyone. I have no friends. Oh yes, I have friends, but no one to whom I can say what I really feel (Mennonite Central Committee Field Report, 1986 cited in Mysliwiec, 1988:60).

One of the more serious consequences for children of family separation, lone parenthood and female headship or female management of households — together with the rise in the population of children — is the reduction in the number of family members available for the care of the very young (UNICEF, 1995).

> Traditionally, as a function of the extended family system in Cambodia, the task of child care would fall to the grandmother living with the family. However, the recent events in Cambodia have assured that there are fewer grandmothers available to provide the continuation of traditional child care systems (Brown, 1994:2).

After widowhood, abandonment or divorce, many people remarry. But step-parenthood can also put children at risk:

> Because men now are marrying again many children are living with step mothers who do not always treat them fairly. This often causes them to run away — they are moving around a lot and doing bad things . . . (Khmer woman working for an international NGO).

> Before 1970 a man who had two or three wives — this was only for the rich men. But now any man can take two or three

wives. This is causing many problems because now the children of the first wife are not liked (Khmer woman working for an international NGO).

Role reversals

Cambodian children have customarily played a part in productive and domestic activities in the countryside. But war has changed both their role within the family and the nature of their interactions with adult relatives. The reversal of the power relation between children and adults under the Khmer Rouge and the forced assumption by children of grave political and social responsibilities has, in the words of one expatriate observer, left many Cambodians with a "residual fear" of children. Some Cambodians believe this accounts for the apparent loss of parental authority over children:

> One Khmer told an aid official that one of the more serious effects of the Khmer Rouge régime was the destruction of the traditional relationships within the family, especially between children and parents. Children who had been separated from their parents and taught to report on them, today no longer have the traditional respect for them (Mysliwiec, 1988:11).

> People have become wild. In the past it was hard to hear people arguing and people wouldn't hurt each other. Young girls could go around anywhere and no harm would come to them. But . . . the children now are terrible, they have no respect for the traditional beliefs. In general people don't respect the monks and nuns and the elderly as they should. Many people mix up what is right and what is wrong, they don't know the difference between sin and not sinning (Khmer nun).

The incomplete nurturing or incomplete support received by children during the Khmer Rouge era undermines their ability, as adults, to provide care to their own children:

> . . . many young adults who today find themselves [as] parents grew up not having had the opportunity to learn by example the skills which they now need . . . . Where the habit of caring is not practised — it is not acquired (Taylor, 1994:28).

Deficiencies in nurture in previous generations are also thought by some to be one of the causes of intra-familial violence:

> The war caused many problems . . . those that are parents now were orphans in the war — they moved around a lot and had no education. They lost their good friends and all they learnt was how to survive. Some became violent just to protect themselves . . . (Khmer man, musician).

The problem is believed to be aggravated by the present economic crisis:

> It is getting worse now because the economy is going down and parents sometimes can't take care of their children so they abandon them. They can go to an orphanage but there they get no discipline. . . . Before 1975 of course there were children who were undisciplined but now it is even worse because during the war there was no school and children were separated from their families (Single mother in Phum Somnagn).

What makes the situation even more difficult is that while destitution increases children's economic responsibilities, and consequently their need for a measure of independence, because of the poor security in many areas parents feel compelled to be far more protective than before. Even the more traditional and apparently innocuous work activities of children, such as collecting firewood or water, can be highly dangerous.

> The thing about the fighting is that they [the government soldiers] just don't care: they shell toward the Khmer Rouge but they don't think of us in the middle. We are in the firing line and it is our fate if we get caught (Women in Banan District).

As a group of Khmer women noted, parents feel obliged to curtail their children's mobility outside the home.

> Children feel afraid to go to the rice field now because of the landmines and the fighting. Before the Pol Pot time we were not rich but we had peace. Security is the biggest problem we face here today . . . we do not let the children go out freely as we used to go as children ourselves because of the landmines and the fighting . . . if only there was peace we could feel free.

Hence an ambiguity in adult-child relations within the family: children exercise a level of responsibility and independence which is seen to go hand-in-hand with a disregard for parental authority and yet at the same time, due to continued violence, parents find they need to exert increased protectiveness and control. It is not known how these tensions are resolved, if indeed they are resolved, or how they affect children's status within and integration with the family.

3.2

Social Change and Demise

Loss of solidarity

We have suggested that, in Cambodia, social networks have traditionally been predicated largely on kinship affiliation, patronage and continuity of residence at the local level. This is not to suggest that community solidarity was strong; notions of community were weak even before the outbreak of conflict and collaboration between members was informal and opportunistic. Subsequent intervention to realign the social fabric has further weakened social alliances and networks, and this has more than likely interrupted social healing. Class was a key factor of vulnerability during the Pol Pot era, when all members of the social élite, the educated and urban dwellers, were singled out for forced relocation, forced labour, or execution. Today, Cambodian refugees cite a Khmer proverb: "When the hollow gourd sinks, the clay pot floats" to draw attention to the fact that at this time people previously at the bottom of the social ladder rose to positions of authority, while those formerly at the top sank to the bottom.

The use of civilians in intelligence gathering had a devastating effect on social alliances, whether outside the family or within: "The Khmer Rouge recruited people to spy on one another. In the place of trust was a terrible fear of being betrayed" (Meas with Healy, 1995:24). As one middle-aged Cambodian man explained:

> People easily become enemies with one another . . . it's difficult to trust one another — even your brothers and sisters. And when we are married there is a problem too. It's almost like we were in different families.

And in the words of a female Cambodian NGO worker:

> During the Pol Pot time they taught us not to trust one another . . . and still now people don't trust each other . . . it's each person for themselves.

Displacement has broken the continuity of residence at the local level and brought people together with complete strangers. Many families are still displaced today, some due to recent disruptions; many have been displaced several times and numerous modern villages contain people only recently settled there. A number of respondents, such as this woman from Battambang, expressed a nostalgia for the past and a concern about the lack of collaboration at the present time:

> Before the Pol Pot time most communities were made up of families and relatives. There was good community spirit then — each person helped the others in the fields. But now there are many new people coming into the community; people don't trust each other (Khmer woman working for an NGO).

We have argued that healing can be facilitated by shared experiences. Collaborative efforts to reconstruct buildings, re-create services and restore previous lifestyles also play a part. The breakdown of social networks and loss of trust isolates individuals, making the collective processing of grief difficult. At the same time, however, it is sometimes suggested that in Cambodia expressing feelings and sharing grief is not culturally appropriate and may therefore not be as important to healing as in other cultural settings. The loss of allies and a sense of solidarity with neighbours and kin are impacts of violence that may somehow seem nebulous and cannot be captured easily in research. Also, it is not easy to anticipate the implications for children specifically. Nevertheless, they undoubtedly have consequences for children — economic and psycho-social — since, at the very least, they reduce the possible options for families and individuals in social or economic distress.

Loss of leadership and moral authority

At one time there was an elaborate, if informal, leadership network at the local level in Cambodia, based largely on religious authority, seniority in age, family prominence, healing powers or other civic skills. The assumption of authority over civilians by the military in Democratic Kampuchea changed the very principles on which leadership had previously been enacted. Violence and corporal punishment rather than self-discipline or social sanction based on collective decisions became the norm during the Khmer Rouge era:

> Insufficient labour input, disobeying orders, theft of food, running away and extra-marital affairs were faults that villagers remember in connection with punishments. This brutal punishment of individual failure contrasted sharply with traditional village life, which had been marked by a high

degree of tolerance of individual behaviour (Uimonen, 1994:11, referring to Ebihara).

The detention, torture or killing of local leaders is a common military tactic because it attacks confidence and instils fear, making it much easier to control and manipulate the populace. By singling out and destroying the most important figures in a village, the very heart of community life is threatened. In Cambodia, particularly invidious was the fact that many of the powerful and important people killed during the Khmer Rouge time were betrayed by fellow villagers:

> Many of the village people, especially the men, died from betrayal. The most respected man in the whole commune was the first to die. All those who had worked for the government were called 'new people' even though they had lived in the village for generations. My father was accused in this way . . . even though he was such a respected man that he is still remembered 20 years later for his goodness. . . .

> All of the respected people in our village were singled out for betrayal. . . . All except one of the 'pious laymen', the *adjar* as they are called, were killed in the pagoda. The one who was spared was in league with the Khmer Rouge . . . (Meas with Healy, 1995:24-25).

A decline in moral authority and leadership in present day Cambodia and the associated corruption in political circles is perceived as a major problem by a significant number of expatriates and Khmer.

> Many Cambodian people detest and abhor the moral degradation which they observe in government circles, but feel powerless to effect the desired changes. For this reason, to some young urban intellectuals even the Khmer Rouge appeal as an attractive alternative (Taylor, 1994:30).

We Khmer who have been trained abroad, we have big values such as the rule of law. But it is difficult to explain it to Cambodians here because they have had three layers of rulers — the Indianized dictatorship, the French dictatorship and the Communist dictatorship. Now it is an uphill task to remove the remnants of the layers of these dictatorships (Male Cambodian returnee, head of local NGO).

Many people argue that the Buddhist monkshood in particular no longer experiences the respect it once enjoyed:

People are not sure that the Theravada Buddhist establishment knows what it is doing; and the many new novice monks are much too young to be able to offer wisdom or words of comfort for those in distress (Taylor, 1994:22).

Monks had to change because they went abroad, their weakness came from outside . . . now when you see a monk, you see a picture of a monk, you don't know whether it is a monk or not (Elderly Khmer man from village in Battambang province).

However, the majority of Cambodians still consult the *kruu Khmer*, as a female street trader in Battambang commented:

Most people here believe in the *kruu Khmer* and my experience with them is good . . . when I get depressed, when my business goes down I go and see a few and compare what they say. If they are similar I take their advice. It's not so much the advice they give me but hope — they give me hope in the future.

Anxiety about insecurity nationally and corruption among senior politicians is pervasive in many circles. As a result, some young people living in Phnom Penh have come to think what for others is unthinkable — that it would be preferable for the Khmer Rouge to resume power; for whatever crimes they committed, at least they knew what they wanted and were not corrupt. Take, for example, the comment made by one young Khmer aid worker in an international NGO:

> Sometimes, I think it would be better if the Khmer Rouge came back because at least then we would know who was in power. Today the government is shared and that can only mean trouble.

Undoubtedly there is a crisis of confidence in civil, and to some extent also religious, leadership in Cambodia today. This crisis is expressed daily in the newspapers and other fora. Some might suggest that the situation is an inevitable effect of importing democracy into a society that has previously only known centralized authoritarian rule or a result of the armed conflict that still festers. For children, it means an absence of well defined, positive moral codes or role models and possibly a loss of spiritual guidance as well.

Destruction of the economic base

Undoubtedly much of the poverty in Cambodia today can be attributed to the long years of conflict and to the more recent economic liberalization policies. Many Khmer Rouge projects were fundamentally defective in design (Mysliwiec, 1988; Ledgerwood, et al., 1994). Small traditional plots were consolidated into large non-terraced fields, resulting in the drying-out of major tracts of land used for growing rice or grazing and the flooding of areas used traditionally for non-flooded crops. The effect was to destabilize production and increase vulnerability to flooding and droughts. Poorly constructed works swept away in floods and permanent changes in water flow patterns meant that even after the downfall of the Khmer Rouge farmers returning could no longer use their past knowledge to predict and control water movement. Records, maps, documentation and agricultural research were all destroyed, along with germplasm collections.

The older Khmer can recall that while everyone was forced to work much harder at this time, they had no control over their produce, which was taken from producers and distributed centrally. Food shortages were acute in many areas; yet eating in private or scaveng-ing for food were prohibited. Communal dining was particularly despised. Many deaths resulted from malnutrition or outright star-vation. And the defeat of the Khmer Rouge did not improve matters much, partly because during their subsequent retreat, they took a quarter of the rice harvest and destroyed any draught animals they could not take with them (Mysliwiec, 1988:11).

There is general agreement in Cambodia today that the changes in the system of production brought about by Pol Pot have had lasting economic effects:

> After the Khmer Rouge period many people moved to the city because they couldn't use the land. . . . Cambodia had become one big mine field and this forced many to the city. People also thought that the city could give them a good life, but they had no skills, they just knew about cultivation, so often they couldn't find work and they became troubled — sick (Khmer woman).

After the downfall of the Khmer Rouge, an embargo of development aid imposed by most major donor governments and drastic cuts to the aid budgets of international organizations were serious impediments to economic recovery under the Vietnamese-backed PKR government.

Most available aid went directly to the border camps rather than to the majority of the population, which remained in Cambodia. As a result, the border operation acted as a magnet, attracting people from within Cambodia. Indeed, the camps also provided sustenance for the forces of the coalition parties, who at the time were not only fuelling the fighting in Cambodia but also disrupting the economy and reconstruction efforts. Lacking technical assistance, developmental support and bilateral aid from Western governments, Cambodia lagged far behind neighbouring countries economically at this time. Despite this, and with the support of several Soviet Bloc and Asian countries and a handful of international non-governmental and multilateral agencies, the PKR did much to stave off massive famine and restore the transport system and administrative infrastructure.

Economic insecurity

The pressure on resources

Cambodians and expatriates often talk about the recent increases in poverty:

> People now are really very poor; in the past if they were poor, they might not have had a good house or clothes to wear but they could eat. Now some people don't even have enough to eat (Elderly man in Phum Somnagn).

The lack of longitudinal data makes it hard to determine whether there really has been a growth in absolute poverty or whether it is more a growth in relative poverty associated with economic liberalization and rising social differentiation. And again, it is not always possible to distinguish a yearning for an ideal past before there was conflict from the reality of pre-war times. Nevertheless, many adverse economic trends can be observed in Cambodia today. Economic stability is threatened by the long-term impact of conflict on tenure and access to land and by economic liberalization and distortion, as much as by population increase. And a good deal of land is rendered unworkable because of landmines.

> The shifting conflict, accompanied by the sterilization of land by mining, and now the re-mining of land which had earlier been de-mined, means less agricultural land is available for use. New land may be found in the forest areas but, given the ever present danger of stepping on a land mine and the difficulty of clearing the land without equipment, it is only the foolhardy and the desperate who try their luck at this option (Taylor, 1994:12).

Landlessness is another major problem. Due to extreme population pressure, 10 to 15 per cent of people in communities near Battambang, for example, are without land (Taylor, 1994). Most of these are internally displaced people. Between 1979 and 1989 land ownership was vested in the state. In land distributions that took place in 1989, rights of ownership were transferred to those working the land. People absent from their homes at the time of the distributions lost their land rights, with the result that many of those returnees without resources of their own remain landless today.

> . . . [after the sharing out of land] most people got a small part of the land but much of the land belonged to the powerful ones. When we got the land the families were much smaller than they are now — now we have many children and it is difficult to feed us all from this land (Khmer woman working for a local NGO).

The government still owns large tracts of land, some of which have been allocated to returnees. However, much government property is in areas that are heavily mined and any returnees with sufficient funds prefer to settle in un-mined areas. Even those with land are forced to live on parcels inadequate in extension to fulfil basic subsistence requirements:

> People have always regarded Battambang as an area with good land, so many more than were originally from Battambang resettled here from the border. But, not only did they find they received much smaller amounts of land than they had expected but landmines and continued fighting restricted their work (Khmer man working for a local NGO).

And a significant proportion of families are landless because of mismanagement or misfortune. Sickness is cited by many as leading to indebtedness and land transfers: first there is the loss of the labour of the sick person; second, there is the cost of medical treatment (Meas with Healy, 1995).

> If people need money to pay for treatment when they get ill they may be forced to sell their land: first the good land, then the not-so-good land. Sometimes people will then rent a while, but more often than not they are still paying back a debt and are unable to pay the rent for it and may finally sell their residential land and move to the city (Khmer man working for a local NGO).

Allocating land to the landless can cause conflict, however, and ownership of land is fiercely contested in some cases: "If they gain land but in doing so become rejected and excluded from the social structure of the village, more is lost than is gained" (Meas with Healy, op.cit.:44). Village leaders and monks noted the difficulty of resolving such disputes, many litigants having to resort to the law. Certainly laws dictating who is eligible for which land do exist, but they do not always help clarify the situation. A Cambodian judge highlighted this:

It is not clear whose land is whose — why should people have taken care of the land during the 1980s if the land was in fact government land. Yet there were of course many claims after the announcement (in 1989), many of them false — people claiming they had worked this or that piece of land which in fact they hadn't been using at all.

Some families are destitute because of a lack of male labour or draught animals. Access to water for irrigation is another critical factor. According to an ILO study (Taylor, 1994:10) all farming families working non-irrigated land suffer from a food deficit of four months per year or more, whereas 82 per cent of farmers with irrigated land suffer food deficits for around three months. Some 60 to 70 per cent of households do not produce half the rice they need for annual consumption and very few sell any rice. Family food consumption constitutes the largest proportion of total cash expenditure.

The changing military and social conditions in many areas of the northwest particularly, oblige an increasing number of people to consider migration to the towns as their only option. A survey conducted by Childhope Asia with the local Phnom Penh Municipality found that 35 per cent of migrants to Phnom Penh come alone. Many end up homeless, others as squatters. Three quarters earn a living by begging. Migration to the city is often seasonal, coinciding with periods of low activity in rural areas. Some take up petty vending, but this can be difficult, as traders in Battambang indicated:

> The economy is not so good these days; it is harder to feed families today. There is very little profit from business. It's probably because of the fighting; people can escape the fighting but they don't spend money. All this moving around, all the changes, it doesn't help business (Khmer street trader, single mother).

Things are harder for me now than when I lived in the village as a rice farmer. I know I didn't have children then, but there you have food all around you. Now I am in the city I have to buy everything. . . . In the past you could sell things and the money you got had value, but today the money doesn't have so much value (Woman trader, Battambang).

We have seen that incessant, grinding poverty can have a debilitating effect on adults, rendering them incapable of providing the kind of nurturing care that children need for their self-esteem and general well-being. In Cambodia, these negative effects of poverty are heightened by the continued threats to security in many areas, making certain important economic activities dangerous or impossible and continuously attacking independence and confidence in the future. Some livelihood strategies entail great risk for adults and children alike:

The poorest people from the villages still go to cut wood in the mountains although now this is extremely dangerous and illegal. They sell it to buy food to support their life. Villagers have died in the mountains because of malaria or mines and the women have been raped by soldiers who are based there (Meas with Healy, 1995:44).

Close to the minefields the situation of the hungry is even worse. They are often willing to scavenge in the minefield for food or for something to sell to buy food. Some types of mine casing can be sold for motor bike spare parts, they tell me, but you have to go in there and disable the mine (ibid.:40).

Poverty also increases susceptibility in children to trafficking, separation from family, loss of access to education and other services and exploitation and danger at the workplace.

As one Cambodian woman put it:

The children of returnees are often made quite vulnerable. For those returnees who accepted money rather than land, when the money runs out they put children to work and often they have to do jobs that they are not capable of.

Phenomena such as child street work have now begun to capture the attention of NGOs and others. As yet, though, information on hazardous child labour in Cambodia is sparse and unsystematic and because of the lack of longitudinal data or case controls, it is not possible to state whether children do work that is either dangerous or exploitative as a result of conflict or the present economic instability or, in other words, whether it represents a deterioration in conditions by comparison with the pre-war years. There is evidence that young teenagers have been recruited for active combat: this is likely to be one of the most hazardous occupations young people in Cambodia engage in. NGOs have started, as far as is feasible, monitoring the numbers and circumstances of underage combatants. However, there needs to be further research on the broader issue of child labour if a policy to reduce psycho-social and physical hazards to children is to be brought into effect.

Criminal activity

For lack of any viable alternatives, as much as for any other reason, a significant number of people faced with destitution resort to crime, corruption or similar activities which are considered in Cambodia to be socially unacceptable.

> The problem now is there is no clear law as to what to do, no law about what to do to people who abuse one another . . . now there is a lot of prostitution and robbing and stealing. You have all these business people and international people coming in and out of the country — you can't tell who is good and who is bad . . . Yes, people were influenced on the border but when the cable television and all the people who have money

to spend came in — that is the worst. I have never seen anything like it before (Male musician in Battambang).

Those families that are fleeing the war are in the most difficult situation. Sometimes they can go to the *wat*. Sometimes they can work for others . . . but often they have to steal and rob, and in these situations it is often the children that are put at most risk (Khmer woman working for an international NGO).

Family destitution is believed to be drawing a growing number of children of ever diminishing age into prostitution. Large numbers of children are also engaged in activities such as street vending which can lead to involvement in crime.

The times now are difficult on children. Girls can easily be taken into prostitution. I am worried someone will take my girls and force them into prostitution. And for the boys there are many street gangs now who are involved in stealing — they are a bad influence on my boys. . . . It is difficult for those children in families where there is no husband. Fathers are more able to keep control of the children than us. Especially the boys . . . they go around and about, here and there, and they can easily get into trouble (Single mother in Phum Somnagn).

As with other economic activities undertaken by Cambodian children that are actually or potentially hazardous, there is so little known about their involvement in crime that any conclusions about negative psycho-social consequences would be highly speculative.

3.3

Cultural Loss

To consciously revise the core of cultural constructs, beliefs and values that in some way manifest a past shared by the Cambodian people is to attack the heart of civil society. There has been widespread exposure to social engineering and cultural reconstruction at the hands of various rulers in Cambodia. Replacing the old order with the new under Pol Pot entailed the elimination of existing religious beliefs and social customs, ensuring unquestioning loyalty to the militarized state: this loyalty was founded on fear and mistrust.

> Khmer culture has at least partially disappeared. Because of the tremendous loss of lives . . . not only dancers, but monks who knew how to chant certain religious texts properly, craftsmen who knew how to construct distinct kinds of ox carts, and women who knew how to weave specific designs perished with their knowledge.

Much of the written documentation on Khmer culture was similarly lost. As a result of the deliberate destruction of texts by the Khmer Rouge, combined with loss from neglect and the effects of the elements, less than half of the Khmer-language materials from before 1975 exist today (Ledgerwood et al., 1994:2).

Theravada Buddhism, Islam and Christianity were ruthlessly suppressed. Buddhist temples, often at the heart of village life, were destroyed and Buddhist monks and nuns killed or forced to break their vows (Ledgerwood et al., 1994:2). Comments made by several Cambodians during fieldwork were imbued with fear for the moral consequences of what is perceived as cultural destruction:

> People have learnt different ways, they are now more likely to be negative than positive, they are now more likely to be violent than merciful (Khmer man).

> The way the war has affected the society [is that when people] . . . might have had a good attitude in the past they now have a bad attitude . . . I find this very difficult, but it's not just that people are more cruel but there is a real problem with the government (Khmer woman).

The replacement of traditional culture and spiritual beliefs by Western norms and values since the UNTAC period has been cited by both Khmer and expatriates as a contributory factor in the weakening of parental authority over children:

> Many people, particularly the younger generation and those living in cities, no longer participate so actively in the traditional Buddhist and cultural practices. There is a move away from Cambodian cultural norms and practices towards a more "Western" approach. This is resulting in parents feel-

ing they have lost control over their children (Harmer, 1995:15).

While it is unlikely that Cambodian culture was ever constructed as a systematic and consensual whole, there is a belief that something that once was shared by all or most Cambodians has been irretrievably lost. Whether or not it in any way reflects reality, this sense of loss invokes both anxiety about the future and nostalgia for the past and entails specific fears in relation to children and their socialization.

3.4

Consequences for the Individual

Psycho-social well-being

As already indicated, the symptoms of psycho-social distress are many and varied. However, there is very little systematic information on this topic in Cambodia, especially with regard to children. What little research does exist has largely been conducted with adult refugees, mainly in the United States, a high percentage of whom exhibit a range of symptoms that within the Western biomedical model are understood to derive from "mental health" problems.

Khmer refugees in resettlement countries experience what has been referred to as the "Pol Pot syndrome": "non-specific pains, insomnia, loss of appetite, palpitations and difficulties in breathing" (Swain, 1985, cited in Ledgerwood et al., 1994). In one survey in California, 84 per cent of Cambodian households reported a member under a physician's care compared to 45 per cent for Vietnamese and 24 per cent for Hmong and Lao (Ebihara, 1985, cited in Ledgerwood et al., 1994)

Bit (1991) cites depression as the single most common complaint among Cambodian patients in the United States. Recurrent thoughts of death and of stressful experiences in Cambodia are common. Sleep patterns are often disturbed and excessive fatigue and energy loss interfere with daily tasks. Conversion disorder, or the loss of specific sensory or motor functions without any organic cause, is also mentioned by Bit as a widespread problem. And a very high percentage of patients experience a range of symptoms which are associated by many with PTSD. Bit maintains that a significant proportion of Cambodians in the United States have developed defence mechanisms such as attitudes of denial or dissociation. Physical expression of these mechanisms was identified in aggressive behaviour towards weaker targets such as family members and avoidance of speaking the Cambodian language or making friends with other Cambodians.

Because of the lack of primary research, most of the information on the psycho-social condition of the population within Cambodia is anecdotal. Nevertheless, psycho-social distress in children and adults is thought to be widespread. Writing with a sense of impending disaster about the young people who were living in Site Two refugee camp in Thailand, Mollica and Jalbert maintained that:

> ... Many Khmer children and adolescents have been highly traumatized, especially the survivors of the Pol Pot children's groups. These young people will attempt to mask their depression and intellectual deficits through denial, indif-

ference, poor school performance and anti-social behaviour. Unless their problems are adequately addressed, they will become dysfunctional adults and eventually place enormous economic and social burdens on their future communities (1989:cited in Utting, 1994:155).

Many people interviewed in Phnom Penh and Battambang during our field research referred to their own emotional or mental health problems and to those of friends, neighbours and colleagues, and much of the literature on Cambodia also touches on the issue. With regard to children specifically, speculation is likely to underestimate the actual incidence of psycho-social distress. Research in several countries shows that when a child experiences distress, this may not be apparent to adults, including parents. Whatever the causal explanation within the Khmer cosmological system and whatever the meaning within Khmer culture, when people in Cambodia refer to their feelings or to their health a variety of "symptoms" familiar to Western science are identified. Sometimes a direct link is made between political conflict and a particular symptom, although often the association is not obvious and poverty seems to be the primary causal factor.

The Kampuchean people continue to suffer not only from physical illness but from unhealed emotional scars left from so many years of oppression, abuse and the loss of family members and friends. . . . The problems manifest themselves through depression and chronic grief, through the recurrence of nightmares, anxiety and fear of being exposed. Other symptoms of this debilitating illness include lack of motivation and difficulty in planning and organizing work, as well as an inability to generate enthusiasm and hope for the future (Mysliwiec, 1988:56).

People often argue that somatic symptoms, depression and other psychological phenomena are especially prevalent in Cambodia. Thus, for example:

> There are many cases of chronic disability, showing up as psychosomatic symptoms such as unremitting headaches, or as anxieties expressed in culturally specific ways such as the somatic experience of being possessed by ghosts or spirits. There are people with symptoms consistent with the diagnosis of PTSD. Psycho-social problems resulting from conflict in Cambodia also have their effect on the social level (IPSER, 1993:5).

And in the words of the Khmer:

> In the Pol Pot time I saw a lot of people who were shocked: they became very exhausted and ate bad food, they had bad feelings. Now you see a lot, particularly women, who are about 35-45 [years old] who get very dizzy still. My aunt is like this — she quite often gets shocked and sometimes she thinks about things too much and she gets dizzy. She can get very nervous. Happiness makes it better but if she sees an accident it can make her very shocked again (Woman working for an international NGO).

> Since that time when I lost my family I have been alone. I can get very bad headaches. If there are problems in the family I can faint. I now have a weak heart. I can't become too happy or too sad, although sadness makes me more sick than happiness.

> Sometimes I see people who are getting worried a lot and this causes pressure on the heart. If you see people beginning to fade away you must beat the heart area many times to bring

them back (A woman healer who lost both her children during
the Pol Pot period).

Anxiety, fear, lack of hope, self-respect or self-esteem and a sense of
guilt or shame affect both adults and children and are recurring themes
in Cambodia. Many suffer lingering fear. Sain from Phum Srai (a
pseudonym) recalls her childhood memories from the time when the
Vietnamese troops were advancing into her home area and the villagers
were summoned into the mountains by the Khmer Rouge shortly
before their eventual flight.

> One day I saw a large pond and I thought that maybe I was
> to be killed, because the pond was full of bones and skulls and
> it smelled very bad. I couldn't sleep for two days, and I missed
> my family. I saw many corpses in the forest also. And people
> who were tied together so they could not run away. One day
> when I was working I had a high fever. I fell into the pond,
> but I managed to get up again. I was very frightened. . . . In
> 1983/84 I had nightmares for a year, maybe two or three
> times every month. When I woke up I felt happy again. In the
> dream my spirit was afraid. Now I have forgotten many things
> about Pol Pot. But when I hear shooting with big guns I'm
> afraid, because then I remember (cited in Uimonen, 1994:17).

One of the more insidious effects of conflict is the feeling of guilt and
lack of self-esteem experienced by survivors, whether they were
innocent bystanders, victims or perpetrators of violence. As one senior
Khmer monk put it: "Many have lost self confidence. They have lost
their inner peace and they don't believe that they can determine their
own lives any longer". Meas Nee also refers to this issue:

> . . . the dignity and pride in our identity, formerly an im-
> portant part of our lives, entirely disappeared. . . .

Self-reliance, hope for the future, and dignity, were drained away (Meas and Healy, 1995:27).

Khmer amputees articulate the shame and lack of self-esteem they associate with their physical condition:

I lost all my sense of being and self-esteem and filled myself instead with cowardice, fear and despair. . . . The words wouldn't stop wringing in my ears "I am an amputee". There is no reason for living found in these words . . . living like a reptile which hides its face when it meets other animals or men, or like the *pralang ka(s)*, a bird that gets its food from the female or like the kind of tree that grows on another tree. That's why others are frustrated and disregard me. I am a parasite . . . I try to encourage myself that my legs and arms will grow back after Cambodia achieves peace and thinks about the social welfare of her people and not about greedy power . . . . So while waiting to grow back my arms and legs, my stomach feels hungry. It shouts for food. I am famished. What will I do to fill my hungry stomach? I will beg, which is full of shame (Hay, 1993).

Victims of political conflict sometimes experience intense anger. But it is the view of some expatriate aid workers that the expression of anger, as with the expression of other strong emotions, is counter-cultural in the context of Cambodia.

People here have little connection to their own emotionality. . . . People here are more physically oriented. When you ask how they feel they say their head aches. The feeling issue and the trauma they have experienced is pushed under the rug . . . people try to move away from feelings issues as fast as they can and they try to forget, people here are taught to forget (Expatriate).

Indeed, it has been suggested that suppressing powerful emotions may be an important coping strategy in Cambodia.

The Khmer people have, for centuries, been accustomed to linking physical with emotional functioning. In addition, the ability to suppress emotions, suffer silently, and be pleasant toward others is highly valued. In fact, the attainment of these virtues is a measure of personal maturity. As Timberlake and Cook wrote, 'The values embedded in this controlled coping style include self-reliance, resignation, self-respect, and suppression of unwanted emotions in order to maintain dignity' (Timberlake and Cook, cited in Bromley, 1987:237).

In line with this, several people note the particular capacity of Cambodians to forgive those who have harmed them:

Many a foreign aid worker in Kampuchea has been impressed and moved by the spirit of forgiveness some Khmers have shown toward those who once inflicted suffering on them during the Khmer Rouge régime (Mysliwiec, 1988:48).

A Khmer also touches on this issue:

You cannot judge someone for what they had to do to survive. I do not seek revenge against the Khmer Rouge. They were peasants; they were ignorant. They did whatever they were told to do without thinking. Besides, if we felt revenge, perhaps there would soon be no more Khmers left in our country (Mennonite Central Committee Report, 1984, cited in Mysliwiec, 1988:48).

The last two and a half decades of political violence in Cambodia surely must have had, and continue to have, major psycho-social consequences for children as well. Social structural and personal distress is everywhere evident and the impacts have been transmitted through the generations, so that children today bear the consequences of their parents' and grandparents' past suffering. Nevertheless, as stated, information about the psycho-social well-being of Cambodian children is even more scarce than information concerning adults. While there is some anecdotal evidence, much of this is merely a bi-product of training courses or health service assessments rather than systematic research. Kinzie et al. (1986) surveyed Cambodian school children in Portland, Oregon and found an extremely high level of exposure to major stressors. According to Bit, eight in 10 children were separated from their family; 98 per cent had endured forced labour; 83 per cent had gone without food for long periods; 43 per cent had seen people being killed — 18 per cent saw their own family members killed; all had seen corpses in their almost 4 years of work-camp experiences (1991:111).

In a survey of the mental health of refugee children in the Thai border camps, Mollica and his colleagues found strong indications of high levels of emotional disturbance. "Traditional" Khmer somatic symptoms of distress were found to be the most common, although the authors argued that the true prevalence of culture-specific psychiatric disorders will not be known until defined for Khmer children in particular. One important finding was that children's somatic complaints were reported far more frequently by children themselves than by their parents. Children were more aware of the traumas than their parents, shelling, bombing and lack of food, water and shelter were the most serious of their problems. The high prevalence of somatic symptoms was also associated with poor social abilities, lower health status and nightmares and correlated closely with the number and kinds of personal traumatic events.

Moral and social impacts

Both Cambodians and expatriate aid workers express a concern about the prevalence today of values, attitudes and practices in Cambodia that were learned — and may even have assisted survival — during conflict, which in peace time are not merely counter-cultural but even socially dysfunctional. Looking to oneself before helping others, for example, can be a protective mechanism enhancing resilience during periods of extreme violence and social upheaval. But as a residual effect of conflict such attitudes can have negative implications for personal relationships and especially for family life:

> People have become individualistic and think only about themselves and only about today. . . . They have also forgotten what it was like in the past when people used to know one another and would solve problems at a community level. People respected the elderly and the monks, the teachers. They would sing and play music and tell folk tales together — harvest together. . . . Today you don't see people doing things together, you don't see the monks offering advice to the young (Cambodian male returnee, head of a local NGO).

Loss of trust is a consequence of political violence in Cambodia mentioned more frequently than many others, and is felt to impede social reconciliation, forgiveness and healing. Meas Nee writes, for example: "As trust was broken we reached a time when we could think only of ourselves and our great needs . . ." (Meas with Healy, 1995:27). And as one woman explained: "The Pol Pot time taught us not to trust one another, now it's each one for themselves".

The greatest concern in terms of moral and social impacts is with criminal and domestic violence and other forms of abuse. These are behaviours associated not just with value distortion but also with lawlessness, poverty and the ready availability of arms in a post-conflict setting. Certainly the evidence from countries like South Africa, El Salvador and Nicaragua suggests that in the aftermath of war criminal violence increases, possibly due to the difficulty of demobilizing soldiers into a labour market with very limited absorptive capacity. Young people skilled only in soldiering are particularly disadvantaged and may resort to violent crime in frustration at the lack of economic opportunity.

> Years of war and violence have resulted in some people being so damaged by their experiences that they no longer have a respect for life. The demobilizing of soldiers, many of whom may never have known "normal" lives, the lack of employment opportunities and the ready availability of weapons, has led to increased violence and lawlessness. It is not clear to what extent, if any, lawlessness exists because of the impact of psycho-social damage on the perpetrators of crime rather than a lack of law enforcement or clear examples of human rights abuses by those in power (Harmer, 1995:15).

> When I was in the United Kingdom it struck me that people never really used violent swear words — they used other swear words but they didn't often convey violence. In Cambodia however we might say: 'don't do that or I'll hit you' if we wanted to be mild, or else we might say 'may lightening strike you dead' and 'may the bullet hit you and kill you dead' or 'may someone chop off your head'. I am sure this contributes to the levels of violence in families (Khmer man, head of local NGO).

However pervasive these violent attitudes, the evidence for domestic violence as being a behaviour learned during political conflict is quite controversial. Apart from anything else, there is no information about its incidence in Cambodia prior to the outbreak of conflict. Moreover, domestic violence occurs in all known societies, including those that have not experienced political conflict.

Unable to cope with stress, some adults resort to alcohol or gambling:

> The poorest are those [families] where the adults are often sick and can't work properly. The extra problem is that some of these very poorest people are now gambling. They have no job. For example, there is this one man who has been trying very hard but now he is in such a bad situation and for the first time I found him drunk. This is the problem of debt. He told me that things were so hard that he just wanted to drink to forget his problems (Community development worker).

Several Khmer explained that the way they deal with extreme stress is to neglect their domestic responsibilities:

> When things have been really bad, when I have no food to feed the children and my husband has been arguing and drinking a lot I just leave. I go to my relatives in the village and I just forget about everything and then I come back after a few days (Street trader in Battambang).

But in many cases a parent, usually the father, may not come back. The following account is from a child that has been internally displaced since returning to Cambodia from the border camps. His family was living in extreme poverty. The child's father had recently left the home, which was an obvious cause of distress to him, and was experiencing severe problems. Although 14 years old, the boy had only ever attended school for two months. He showed signs of severe malnutrition, with a bloated stomach and discolouring of the hair.

Boy living in Phum Somnagn:
"I arrived in this place about a year ago. Because there was a lot of fighting we had to leave the place where I was living before and walk here, staying close to the road side. I never knew much about that place because my mother would not let me go out much because of the landmines, but I do remember that close by to my house there was a banana field and sugar palm trees. There my mother used to work as a labourer digging ponds and building roads for rice. I used to see the tanks moving about a lot on the hill above my house.

"After a while on the border I started school, but it only lasted two months because then we came to this district. I used to sell gasoline that my father got from the trucks — he used to drive the trucks. [When asked what his father was doing now he was quiet for a while and cried. After a time he continued. . . .]

"My father went to Sisophon to be with another woman. Now I am just with my mother and I help her to sell the cakes. I go to the soldiers' base to sell the banana rice cakes that my mother makes. She fries the cakes at home and then wraps them in banana leaves — then I sell them for 100 riel a piece. Sometimes the soldiers are bad and eat the cakes but don't pay me. Some of the soldiers' children go to the school in the village.

"I cannot go to school because it would cost me 3,000 riel a year [US $ 1.20]."

3.5

Who Is Most Vulnerable?

Vulnerability analysis

In an attempt to identify patterns of social disadvantage and social distress in Cambodia, as well as to rationalize the use of resources so that the most needy can benefit from interventions, the aid community is gradually developing a framework based on the notion of social vulnerability. A series of vulnerable categories have been marked out as a priority for targeted assistance, on the grounds that they constitute the most economically marginal, or the most exploited and stigmatized members of society.

That there are a large number of vulnerable groups in Cambodia today is understood to be a direct result of the long years of violence and economic decline and of the kinds of survival behaviours mentioned previously as being dysfunctional during peace time. Thus, it is said that the: "large numbers of women and children living on the streets, of young girls sold as labour or prostitutes, of increasing domestic violence and polygamy are some of the more obvious symptoms of social disintegration of families" (Harmer, 1995:14). A few of these social categories embrace whole families — female headed or female managed families, for example. A few are constituted exclusively by adults, such as elderly people without relatives, and some by children — street children, for instance. Regarding children, the main concern currently are those trafficked and/or sexually exploited, those involved in combat, and street, orphaned and unaccompanied children.

While vulnerability analysis based on categorization of this nature has many advantages, such classifications are not unproblematic. Among other things, they risk stereotyping and secondary stigmatization. As Taylor notes, it is easy to make false assumptions by building on stereotypes:

> A person may be at the same time a returnee, an internally displaced person, a widow, a head of household without male labour, a person with many young children, a landless labourer, and a war invalid. Not all people falling within any or even all of these and similar categories would necessarily be classified as poor by the standards of the society around them. The more categories one occupies, the greater are the chances of arriving in the poor house. Yet special circumstances sometimes apply: a person may be receiving remittances from relatives abroad, for example (Taylor, 1994:10).

Being labelled "vulnerable" may not accurately reflect individual experience. An international aid worker highlighted this:

> During last year's Peace March we were caught in some cross-fire in which a monk and a nun were killed and others

injured. As I lay in a ditch with shelling overhead the Monk I was lying beside told me about how important it was to him to be home — how being elsewhere controls your life. 'Even this is better than being in the camps' he told me: 'at least here we can run when we want, we don't have to wait for the UN to tell us to. Although life may have been easier there — we could get food and medical care — here we can do what we want to, when we want to'.

The concept "vulnerable group" is very static. In practice, many of the individuals who are defined as belonging to a socially marginalized group drift in and out of different living situations, entering different social categories as they do so. In most countries the majority of street children, for example, live on the streets only intermittently, returning home regularly, as well as entering custodial institutions from time to time. Moreover, use of the term "vulnerable" implies a social passivity and dependence in those affected. But research internationally with street and working children as well as with children affected by armed conflict has provided strong evidence of their resourcefulness and independence of spirit. Adversity can have its benefits, as some Cambodians acknowledge:

> During the Pol Pot time I became stronger, I learnt to survive
> — to grow things — to find food — to become smart. For me
> I became stronger with more responsibility during that time
> (Khmer woman).

The most vulnerable children

The sexual exploitation of children is a phenomenon which has long been present in Cambodia, although it has more recently been associated specifically with conflict and the influx of foreigners during the UNTAC period. Certainly the sexual exploitation of children is a serious issue in Cambodia today, and foreigners clearly contributed to the rise in demand, although informed sources noted that the poverty-driven supply was already growing in 1991 (Taylor, 1994). Girls in their early to mid-teens are at special risk. Some 10,000 teenage girls and young women are estimated to be in prostitution in Phnom Penh alone, a dramatic increase since 1989 (Taylor, 1994:18). According to an international agency involved in monitoring the situation, Battambang and Siem Riep are two other major areas of prostitution. This could indicate a link with conflict-induced poverty, although further research is needed to verify such an assertion.

The routes into the sex trade are various. Girls are sometimes "adopted" by Cambodian families and then sold into prostitution (de Monchy, 1991). Surveys in a number of provinces of sex workers, pimps, brothel owners, and key informants from the NGO and medical communities, among others, indicated that most girls and young women enter prostitution because of poverty or deception (Human Rights Vigilance of Cambodia, 1995). Most of those in the latter category are deceived not by strangers but by people they know and trust. Some become prostitutes to help their impoverished and indebted families. Many drift into prostitution after running away from home because of domestic violence or similar problems.

Prostitutes working in one area usually come from another province and are therefore cut off from their families. They work from brothels, coffee shops, massage parlours, bars, hotels, restaurants and small rented rest houses.

Recently there has been an alarming increase in reported cases of abduction in Cambodia, mainly of young girls. It is likely that a significant proportion of abductions are for illicit sexual purposes, or for sexual exploitation. Many girls are sold by parents or other relatives to brothel owners, although some may be trafficked into domestic service. Several female students who have disappeared are presumed to have been kidnapped by prostitution rings and countless young girls are sold to brothels in Thailand, travelling via Koh Kong (de Monchy, 1991). Abduction and trafficking are a source of anxiety for local people in Battambang:

> In the last few years there have been a number of cases of girls going missing from Phum Somnagn . . . we know they are going into prostitution. One was lucky, her brother found her before anything happened and brought her back (Woman in Phum Somnagn).

Children in Battambang share these fears, as one 12 year old girl notes:

> When my mother was pregnant with my younger sister we moved to Battambang for a while, but I didn't like it so much as I like it here. . . . The thing about kidnapping is that the kidnappers can give you a toy to play with to lead you away and I have also heard that there may be a chemical in the hands of the kidnapper which could make us follow them.

A boy expressed similar anxieties. He talked about his life in the refugee camp. When asked what he disliked, he went very quiet. Later, when with a group of friends, he said that he was frightened that he would be kidnapped. He had also been frightened when he saw the demon that came out of the top of the tree, saying that he had seen it as he was running away from his home that night. All the other children agreed that it would be extremely frightening to see the demon, but that luckily none of them ever had.

Orphanhood has grave personal consequences for children. However, in most conflicts surprisingly few children are made full orphans as a consequence of violence. Orphanhood as a social concept in Cambodia, however, is not restricted to children whose parents have both died since it tends to include abandoned or separated children as well, and children lacking one parent, normally the father (whether because of death or marital breakdown). The statistics on orphanhood are incomplete. UNICEF maintains, though, that "an unusually high number of children continue to be orphaned and abandoned in Cambodia" (1995:132). The government estimates that there were some 200,000 orphans in the country in 1994, and a 1991 report drawing on information from district leaders in the 11 most populated provinces showed that 1 in 13 children had lost one or both parents (UNICEF, 1995:132). In the Khmer Rouge time many children were separated from their families, although a large number were taken in by other families to have them work in exchange for food (de Monchy, 1991). During war or peace, children are sometimes abandoned as a result of poverty and lone parenthood. Step-children are also at risk of abandonment. The physical separation of children from their families in Cambodia today thus has as much to do with social and economic causes as with conflict.

Most orphans and abandoned children in Cambodia live outside institutions. Even so, UNICEF estimated in the late 1980s that there were some 5,540 orphans living in orphanages; approximately 188,000 were living with relatives at this time (Taylor, 1994:17). The number in institutions has now fallen to 2,397, according to the government (UNICEF, 1995). There is a tradition of adoption in Cambodia linked with the loss of family members. It is common, for example, for childless widows to adopt a child, usually a niece or nephew, as a means of support (Uimonen, 1994). Adoption also takes place among couples with children — as a way of providing for orphans.

Among orphaned children outside institutions "the risk factors for abuse, neglect and exploitation appear to be directly related to the number of relatives who exist, are present and are able to provide care and protection" (de Monchy, 1991:3). Thus, it follows that the minority of orphaned children without any living relatives who are prepared to take them on are the ones most vulnerable. Providing for orphans is a problem, though, especially nowadays ". . . as there are less family members to rely on and often a lack of resources to spare for one more child" (UNICEF, 1995:132). As noted, orphaned girls are at particular risk of being sold. And adoption of children aged over 5 or 6 is more like sale for bonded domestic service (UNICEF, 1995).

Currently, according to UNICEF, there are 5,000-10,000 children on the streets of Phnom Penh (1995). Key informants interviewed by de Monchy said that street children often wander from province to province, some having been sent by parents to generate income. In the Childhope Asia study it was found that most of the children working and/or living on the streets in Phnom Penh were rural to urban migrants. Most of those separated from their families left their homes because of poverty, aggravated by family breakdown and loss of family support, both emotional and financial. One third were found to have no contact with their families. This percentage is far higher than for most other developing countries. Nevertheless, the majority of children on the streets in Cambodia were found to be there for work only and not because they were homeless. Begging is the most important activity for street children, followed by scavenging, vending and portering in the markets. These children have little or no access to services other than those provided by NGOs and a government residential re-education centre for prostitutes. A high proportion are subject to sexual exploitation.

It has already been noted that several international agencies in Cambodia are trying to monitor the numbers and circumstances of child combatants. Recruitment of children under 15 is reported to be a problem, especially in the hill tribe areas of north-west Cambodia (Licadho). Child participation in combat to some extent reflects the very direct way in which the Khmer Rouge involved children in violence, as well as their continued policy of recruiting children today.

But there is some evidence that children are also fighting on the government side. Even though the age limit for recruitment in Cambodia is officially 18, aid workers maintain that children from the government forces are to be found among the wounded in the hospitals. And research shows that the children of government soldiers are militarized by default. In a survey of 77 Cambodian soldiers by The Vietnam Veterans of America Foundation (Roberts and Williams, 1995), just over half were married and a quarter of these were living with their families in the militarized zone (the forests lying between Khmer Rouge strongholds and residential areas). The children of soldiers are vulnerable to shelling, ambush and mines because they live near the front line, help out in the army camps and take food and other supplies to their fathers on the battle field.

Some of the children entering the government forces below the age of 16 do so to aid family survival. Three quarters of the Vietnam Veterans of America Foundation sample were recruited under 20 years of age, and 43 per cent between 10 and 16. Recruitment by village is organized on a lottery basis by the village leader. Random conscription is also common in villages prone to Khmer Rouge intervention. Apparently, some concessions are made to the lack of maturity of conscripts under 16 years of age, since in their first year of service at least they are most likely to do portering behind the front-line (Roberts and Williams, 1995:4). However, children without relatives in the army are not well looked after or protected "One such boy of 12 told us that his overriding fear was of being left behind during an attack on account of not being able to run as fast as the adult soldiers" (Roberts and Williams, 1995:4).

Vulnerability in families

A growing interest in gender issues has led a number of agencies to conduct studies and mount programmes with vulnerable groups of women or lone parent households headed or managed by women. As mentioned previously, women may be left alone because of abandonment, accidental or planned separation, the migration of partners or widowhood. For various reasons, women in Cambodia who raise children without a partner are susceptible both economically and socially and lone women heading families with a high dependency ratio (with many small children and/or chronically sick members) are under particular economic pressure. Female victims of domestic violence are also susceptible, and as already noted, are understood by the aid community to be significant in number in Cambodia. To the extent that lone parent households headed or managed by women include children and to the extent that they are likely to be socially and economically marginal, this kind of family form can present certain direct risks to children.

Many of the expatriate aid personnel presently working in Cambodia first became involved in the country as contributors to the relief effort in the Thai refugee camps. This was a time when displaced and refugee communities took priority in aid programming. Accordingly, some of the most detailed reports on social vulnerability among Cambodians today refer to refugees, returnees and the internally displaced, although these sources rarely give prominence to the circumstances and condition of children in these families.

After the collapse of the Khmer Rouge régime and before the UNTAC period there were many people displaced internationally. A small number of these people managed to obtain official refugee status and a few subsequently settled in countries of asylum. Most, however, remained in camps in Thailand until April 1992, when they began to return to Cambodia — if not to their homes. Each returnee family received assistance in the form of a resettlement grant or land (usually a smaller area than required for self-sufficiency), tools, building materials and food aid, which was allocated for a period of up to 400 days. According to UNHCR statistics, there are now 360,000 returnees in the country, of whom well over half have settled in the Battambang area.

Internal displacement is also a serious problem in Cambodia and internally displaced people now number around 85,000. Since displaced people are ineligible for the international assistance available to returnee refugees, they tend to be worse off economically (UNICEF, 1995). A significant proportion of those displaced internally became so after the UNTAC period when they returned from Thailand to find they had been allocated land which for one reason or another could not viably be cultivated. A major offensive in the north-west between April and May of 1994 forced a further wave of people to flee their homes or temporary camps. Many have been relocated to places where earning a living is virtually impossible, and are thus dependent on NGOs for survival.

Sources of vulnerability in both returnees and internally displaced people include lack of access to resources, such as irrigated land or credit, and poor security. The original resettlement package offered to returnees by UNHCR had included land, although later other options, specifically cash and/or building materials, were made available instead. This was mainly because UNHCR had difficulty in securing sufficient land; indeed when land was allocated it was frequently of poor quality or in unsafe areas. Some families were used as a "buffer" for other local residents — having been located in areas that flood or are insecure. In October 1992 more than 70 per cent of returnees had taken up the cash option, preferring to make their own resettlement arrangements (Davenport et al., 1995; Geiger, 1993). Most resettlement sites are near to an established village, and share its authority structure. In some cases returnees were settled in existing communities, causing resentment among local people who perceive returnees as having run away from the conflict to lead a privileged existence abroad (Expatriate woman who had worked in an NGO in the camps on the Thai border).

The following account is an example of the circumstances of families displaced within Cambodia today.

Displaced woman in Phum Somnagn:
"The oldest child we have is 10 and the youngest 18 months. To survive my husband collects potatoes to sell for rice, but sometimes we receive help from the agencies. We have been here [Phum Somnagn] since April 1994 and as I have small children I have not returned. There is a lot of fighting going on there and I am frightened to return — to see all that fighting again . . . it's difficult. We still have land there and some of my relatives go back and work on the land when it is safe. I had hoped to go back in the dry season but I hear rumours that there will be a big fight.

"We face many difficulties here; we have no equipment as we left all of it behind and this year we had no harvest because we had to flee. Almost everyone here is sick, many of us get dizzy and we have rashes. The children could go to school, but many can't because they are too hungry and too busy finding food. From a very young age children help with collecting vegetables, potatoes and wood. The problem with getting firewood to sell is that they must travel far, and there are landmines there. Children have to work harder today than when I was a child, but we need them to, we need to survive. It's not easy. But we help each other, I borrow from them one day and they from us the next. Now it is the fishing season and I could do something but I have no net.

"It is difficult to say who is in the most difficult situation here; the elderly, the widowers, the families with only young children or those affected by the floods? All of us who have fled are in the same situation here. All we can do is wait for the harvest and hope that we can get money from people by helping them . . . that is if there is a harvest."

PART 4

Understanding and Intervening in Conflict

Monks traditionally assist individuals and families in dealing with problems.
Credit: UNICEF/CP92/1-#71/ Roger Lemoyne.

4.1

Perceptions of Psycho-Social Distress

The question of scale: Views from outside

Many of the members of the expatriate community in Cambodia consider psycho-social issues to be an important priority: "... you get three expatriates together for more than an hour and it comes down to these questions [of psycho-social impact]". When referring to Cambodian history in recent decades, foreigners often use powerful words like "genocide" and "mass trauma". Most perceive psycho-social damage to be widespread:

> Living with years of uncertainty and insecurity has created a population which suffers from what is best described as a collective neurosis. Most people find it impossible to contemplate tomorrow: there is little hope, no expectation and no thought of what one needs to do — or what one could do — to address one's present predicament. Sitting back and waiting for who knows what is all that most people are capable of (Taylor, 1994:28).

Along with several others, Bridget Emerson argues that this trauma, which she defines as encompassing a range of negative social consequences rather than merely the physical symptoms of exposure to violence, serves as a barrier to development in Cambodia:

> Feelings of powerlessness, crushed confidence, and an inability to envision and plan for a more positive future, are common amongst underprivileged groups world-wide concerning the impact of exposure to conflict upon morale, and the ability to cope and plan, it is probable that these impacts may compound the vulnerable feelings of those already in poverty (Emerson, 1996:11).

Emerson mentions reduced confidence, initiative, trust and decision-making and planning skills alongside hopelessness, disillusion, reduced participation, social isolation and an inability to define one's own needs as some of the social consequences defining trauma.

Cambodians, on the other hand, do not always seem to pay as much attention to these issues as might be expected given the enormity of events in recent decades. The NGO Krom Akphiput Phum recently conducted a participatory exercise with a village in Banan district to determine what their problems and needs were. Out of just over 250 families, 18 were returnees. Together they identified their most pressing problems as those we might associate with rural poverty everywhere, regardless of whether or not it is associated with conflict. Problems identified included: the lack of food; shortage of land and fertiliser; too many children; too few draught animals and frequent sickness. All these were seen to cause indebtedness, an overriding concern for everyone. The village is located in one of the most dangerous areas of Cambodia, and yet while people talked about security problems, they mentioned the everyday resource problems outlined above far more frequently. The recent floods, problems to do with schooling and "bad attitudes" — referring to people's cruelty — were also raised.

Is it simply that the Western mental health profession provides the language and the means to isolate and highlight psycho-social distress while such concepts are missing in Khmer? Or is it that expatriates have exaggerated or even stereotyped the problem in Cambodia? These are questions to which there are no obvious answers. Expatriates sometimes account for the apparently low level of concern among the Khmer about psycho-social distress as a matter of culture, or the cultural suppression of difficult or painful feelings, a "trait" we have already mentioned:

> Too many of the traumas here are hidden. This is one of the problems for the future of Cambodia. Closing your eyes to the problem may be based on the traumas which have not been integrated into people's lives. People tell you their whole story in detail when you talk to them as a foreigner. But they don't talk to each other. Everyone has suffered loss so no one can validate their own loss — no one sympathizes because they have all been through the same kinds of terrible experiences (Expatriate man working for a local NGO).

Indeed, the "culture of silence" has been offered by some as an explanation for the prevalence of somatization in Cambodia:

It is believed that somatization is particularly prevalent in cultures where expression of emotional distress in psychological terms is traditionally inhibited, such as in Cambodia, where a high value is placed on interpersonal harmony rather than expression of dissatisfaction or upset. Although not specifically a condition associated with post trauma, psychological stress may well manifest itself physically (Harmer, 1995:3-4).

Several expatriate observers acknowledge, however, that the separation of psycho-social damage from material and economic problems is a false construct of the aid community and runs contrary to the more holistic world view of Cambodians. Dr. Heigel, who at one time worked with Cambodian refugees in the Thai camps, endorsed a more unified approach. He ". . . was convinced that it was not possible to separate psychiatric from a host of other disorders that afflict people, just as it is not possible to separate even urgent medical needs from the basic necessities of food, water and shelter". Heigel maintained that: "The intellectual control of most diseases turns physicians into technicians for the restitution of organ functions while disregarding the fundamental human oneness" (Drucker, 1986:3). The *kruu Khmer's* approach to psycho-social problems on the other hand provides the kind of holistic focus that Heigel maintains is generally ignored by physicians.

Some expatriates are concerned that the preoccupation of the foreign community with the psycho-social consequences of conflict may in fact deflect attention from issues of greater priority to Cambodians:

PTSD is being defined by people from outside, it was created outside by researchers. It is so frustrating, there has been so much research here on this, frustrating because the actual issue is the floods and the droughts and the landmines. The real issues are the economic ones (Expatriate working for an international aid agency).

Psychiatrist Maurice Eisenbruch, on the other hand, does not accept the primacy of economic issues. Nor is he comfortable with PTSD diagnoses. He argues instead that the central problem is the disruption to cultural and religious values among displaced populations or among people forced by military rulers to abandon customary beliefs and rites, causing what he identifies as cultural bereavement (Eisenbruch, 1991a:3; Metraux, undated). Cultural bereavement is associated with the loss of social structures, cultural values and self-identity. It is typified by a tendency to live in the past. The bereaved may be visited by supernatural forces from the past while asleep or awake, or feel guilty about abandoning their homeland. They may experience pain due to the fading of memories of their life prior to the conflict or, in contrast, distressing images of the past may constantly intrude into their daily existence. They may also yearn to complete obligations to the dead or be stricken by anxieties, morbid thoughts and anger that hamper their ability to get on with their daily lives. Eisenbruch stresses that this is not a disease, but an understandable response to catastrophic loss of social structure and culture. Religious faith and participation in religious gatherings are, in his view, important antidotes to this condition.

Finding common ground

Finding a conceptual framework for interpreting and explaining psycho-social distress in Cambodia is undoubtedly a difficult task. The framework with which expatriate aid workers are familiar is entirely foreign to most Khmer. Since it is indeed true that the psycho-social discourse originated and remains in the colonial languages of Europe, even the terms are alien to the Khmer. For example, expatriate staff from the Institute for Psycho-Social and Socio-Ecological Research (IPSER), noted that after years working in Cambodia they are still unable to find an adequate translation for the term "psycho-social". And Gerber and Brown learned when teaching Western mental health concepts and therapeutic approaches that Cambodian trainees had not been exposed to this kind of material before:

> Not only was it literally and figuratively foreign information to them, but they felt that this material did not apply to the Cambodian people and culture. This included material on post-traumatic stress reactions (Brown and Gerber, 1992).

Even among expatriate aid workers there is a confusion about what the term actually means: some use it to refer to strictly mental health matters while others employ a broader definition, referring also to behavioural, moral and social concerns. More rarely the term has incorporated social structural concerns as well. Bit (1991) does not question the relevance of Western concepts and models for Cambodia so much as acknowledge that the lack of familiarity with these concepts is an obstacle to diagnosis:

> Early attempts to assess the presence of PTSD in Cambodian victims were hampered by the difficulty of practising cross-cultural psychiatry with a population that has no experience with Western concepts of mental health. As methods of assessment and understanding of cultural norms and practices have gradually become more relevant to the population, the true dimensions of PTSD in relation to Cambodians have become apparent. Kinzie (1986), for example, believes that virtually all victims of the Khmer Rouge period suffer from PTSD (Bit, 1991:114).

Yet, if familiarity with PTSD diagnosis in Cambodia leads to the kind of generalization made by Kinzie it is not at all evident that anything useful will follow in terms of intervention. At times, the aid community, convinced that indigenous beliefs are inferior to those originating in Western scientific tradition, simply ignores them, importing concepts and ideas without proper explanation and contextualization.

> Most white people think we need to teach them (Khmer people), but we only teach them what we know — we should try to find their way to do things. It is difficult not to see yourself as an expert. We need to forget our own power — although I do know that is difficult . . . Westerners will never, never, never, understand their way of thinking. Some people say to me they don't think but it is just that their process for thinking is very different to ours. It's not logical and takes time to link into (Expatriate working in an international NGO).

The *kruu Khmer*, though, can offer many advantages for Cambodians in need of help:

> Not even the Western model can explain what has happened here. Traditional healers can be excellent counsellors, very progressive and astute and although they can't explain why the things that happened in the Pol Pot time happened, they can explain and rationalize the stuff that happened as a result: they explain it through bad karma and astrology. In Buddhism — it is just the way it is, whilst we labour it much more, we feel guilty and responsible. . . . And we must also remember that it was only 4 years and that does not undo everything that came before (Independent expatriate consultant).

Drawing on external models without assessing real problems and real need, as perceived by Cambodians themselves, carries the risk of creating a serious discontinuity between the need and the aid response:

Most helping organizations package and deliver their benefits in the form of projects or programmes: it is financially and administratively convenient and everyone, except usually the intended beneficiaries, is familiar with the concept. So long as the needs of the community correspond with what the agency offers, or so long as the community spokesperson can be persuaded that what is on offer is what they want, the resources are disbursed and everyone is happy. Unfortunately, the most important needs of a community, as interpreted by the members themselves, rarely correspond exactly with what the agency presumes will be useful (Taylor, 1994:23).

In the consultations that were part of the UNRISD research programme on The Challenge of Rebuilding War-torn Societies, a clear difference emerged in the perceptions of expatriates and Cambodians. Challenged with identifying specific behaviours or coping mechanisms as either "healthy" or "unhealthy" responses to conflict, members of the working group could not agree, the two cultural interpretations being very distinct (Harmer, 1995). As we have noted, "unhealthy" coping mechanisms were defined as attitudes and behaviours that are in some way dysfunctional:

Following long periods of stress, it is inevitable that people develop survivor behaviours which are necessary coping mechanisms during the time of trauma. They may not be conducive to constructive rehabilitation, however, and may be difficult to unlearn once people's lives have become more stable (Harmer, 1995:4).

Unresolved feelings of rage, guilt, betrayal and sadness, for example, were felt to correspond with dysfunctional behaviours such as conflict within the family, lies, excessive alcohol use, violence, divorce and feelings of dependency and helplessness. Some of the more specific issues proved extremely controversial, however: while the expatriates were quite clear about what they saw as unhealthy mechanisms, the Cambodians did not always agree with these classifications. There was a major disagreement, for example, concerning the custom of delivering daughters to urban families for a sum of money so that they could work as servants, which expatriates saw as dysfunctional or exploitative but Cambodians viewed as beneficial to both the children and their families. Possibly one of the obstacles to agreement was the use of terminology, such as "dysfunctional" and "unhealthy", which appears implicitly, if not intentionally, judgmental: such terms have the effect of stigmatizing Cambodian values and practices.

Indeed, it is possible that foreigners dwell disproportionately on issues of vulnerability and pathology in Cambodia: little attention is being paid to the resilience of families and individuals everywhere who have survived with great fortitude the atrocities of over two decades. Many of the informal coping mechanisms developed in Cambodia have very positive impacts on vulnerable individuals: sometimes these are not fully taken into account by the international community. For example, the majority of orphans and abandoned children are provided for by family members and relatives, who also assume responsibility for children they feel are uncared for or at risk (de Monchy, 1991). And as Man Hau Liev comments, children sent as servants to urban areas often benefit not only from exposure to a wider environment and new social interaction but many also learn skills, such as sewing or arithmetic or even the running of a small stall. These skills can be of benefit to the children when they return to their village (Man Hau Liev, personal communication). Informal adoptions of healthy infants are common — new-borns and girls being in particular demand — and Buddhist temples take in young boys who are abandoned or orphaned. More needs to be learned about coping and resilience in Cambodia. Further research should yield more information specifically on the mechanisms that protect children.

Cambodian perceptions of pathology

As yet there is little systematic evidence of Khmer perceptions of pathology in the areas defined by Western science as mental health or social behaviour. Further work needs to be done in this field if the psycho-social interventions of the international community are to be both appropriate and effective. Studies by Eisenbruch (1991a; 1991b; 1994) and Mollica et al. (undated) are of assistance in this regard, as is some of the research conducted with Cambodians in the United States, for example the work of Bit (1991).

Despite the paucity of information, it is evident that for a significant proportion of Cambodians, as well as for many aid workers and academics, the Khmer Rouge régime represented the greatest social catastrophe in Cambodia in living memory. Even though the régime lasted a mere 4 years, it is perceived to be the cause of most of Cambodia's present ills — regardless of the extremely disruptive effects of more recent events. During our fieldwork, several expatriate aid workers expounded theories about the causes of armed conflict in Cambodia. A passive acceptance of authoritarian rule was posited as one explanation:

> The Khmer Rouge merely reflect what was already here in Cambodian society anyway. They are just an exaggeration of what was here before. The Cambodian people have always lived under a strong authority, so they didn't try and fight the Khmer Rouge (Expatriate working in an international aid agency).

And, similarly:

> You know that the way things are now pre-date the Khmer Rouge time. There is no word in Khmer for "citizen", the closest is "subject". People don't participate in the

government, they serve in it. The feudal system still domi-
nates — people accept and are tolerant of powerlessness
(Head of an international NGO).

By contrast, Cambodians tend to define the violence of the Khmer
Rouge régime as something abnormal or extraordinary, something
outside the realm of the normal Cambodian experience. For example,
Uimonen found that several people in a village in Pursat forwarded a
genocide explanation of the Khmer Rouge time. "The Pol Pot period
stands out as 'bad history', whereas the succeeding régime is perceived
as one of 'liberating normalization'" (Uimonen, 1994:24). Thus,
Sawa, a 68-year old farmer, said:

> I hate the Pol Pot period . . . I'm very angry. Pol Pot was very
> bad; treated people like animals. There wasn't enough food
> — people were hungry and malnourished. Many people were
> lost. I don't know why they did what they did. Maybe the plan
> was to kill all people, because even the monks were killed.
> They treated all people like enemies. I don't know who the
> Khmer Rouge are, what their thinking is. They speak the same
> language as Khmer, but they have a bad idea (cited in
> Uimonen, 1994:9).

Thus, Uimonen argues,

> The Khmer Rouge were talked about as a separate political
> faction as well as cultural deviants. . . . The ideas that were
> put into practice during Khmer Rouge rule were evaluated
> according to existing ideas about Khmer culture and the local
> cadres were interpreted as personifications of a new order,
> evaluated as being unsuitable as well as abnormal (Uimonen,
> 1994:12).

Defining the enemy as being in some sense foreign to Cambodia has helped some people cope and come to terms with the atrocities. An elderly woman from the same village commented:

> Maybe the big plan of the Khmer Rouge was to kill all the people. They don't like the people of Cambodia to live in this country. Maybe they want to exchange for another people, maybe the Chinese want to come and live here instead (cited in Uimonen, 1994:13).

Expatriates sometimes view in a critical light the way in which Cambodians externalize their problems. Jennar argues that they: "have a tendency too often to blame all ills on others" (1992:8; see also Bit, 1991). He explains that one of the most successful tactics of the Khmer Rouge was to attribute all the evil and suffering endured by Cambodians during their rule to the Vietnamese. The Vietnamese were again targeted by the Khmer Rouge during the UNTAC period, in what was tantamount to a campaign of ethnic cleansing. As the UNTAC authorities had no mandate to protect the civilian population, they did not intervene. It was observed during our fieldwork that even today many social ills are ascribed to the Vietnamese.

4.2

Framing Psycho-Social Consequences

Explaining the events is one thing, but interpreting their effects on individuals, families and communities is another. As suggested above, there is a lack of fit between indigenous and Western thinking. While Western health systems may make a clear divide between diseases of the mind and diseases of the body, Cambodian conceptions of health are entirely holistic: "Psychological problems are not perceived to be separate phenomena but a reflection of the bodily state of being. Symptoms are described as having a physical manifestation, representing an imbalance in some internal organ" (Bit, 1991:102). Another difference, already described, is that in the Cambodian world view, the path of cause and effect encompasses the individual, his or her social environment, as well as the world of spirits, deities and ancestors. Thus, according to Cambodians, most human experience is determined by the intervention of powerful outside forces, social and supernatural, rather than by individual volition. "It is thus in the area of insight into causal factors and individuation of the self that the Cambodian personality differs from Western perceptions of personality development" (Bit, 1991:98).

But what do these differences mean for those planning psycho-social interventions in Cambodia? Certainly there is a feeling that the sheer scale of what has happened in the country goes beyond the normal scope of therapies, whether these are framed within a Western or Cambodian cosmology. One expatriate who worked in the Thai border camps observed that even the traditional healers have been constrained to explain or give meaning to these events. This leads many people either to turn to imported models or to vacillate between Western and Cambodian theories. PTSD diagnoses appear to offer an obvious and easy solution because they come with ready-made lists of symptoms and with complex problems packaged in a neat syndrome which requires no further interpretation or investigation: "We [the agencies and the people of Cambodia] need a framework to understand what's happened. PTSD gives people that framework" (Expatriate woman working in an international agency).

Nevertheless, while some Cambodians are comfortable with consulting Western practitioners, Western concepts and scientific interpretations have been found, even by their adherents, of little value in helping many others. Brown and Gerber (1992), for example, were motivated to undertake a field study of the culture, religion and world view of Cambodians precisely because they had observed that Western psychologists and mental health practitioners working with Khmer refugees in the United States were having very limited success. Likewise, Vail (1993) notes how the most common health complaint among the *Kreung*, a Mon-Khmer highland group living in north-eastern Cambodia, is being "out of energy", a condition that has proved entirely elusive to medical practitioners trained in Western theory. Extensive examination frequently yielded no workable diagnosis and in many cases no other symptoms could be solicited verbally.

Not all expatriates are happy with using the instruments of Western medicine. Summerill (undated) laments the use of diagnostic instruments for psycho-social stress which have not been culturally validated for Cambodians. Conceding that the Harvard Trauma Questionnaire is one of the most culturally developed diagnostic models for measuring symptoms associated with PTSD, she notes that this is merely because it includes additional questions that try to address symptoms derived from Cambodians' specific experiences. In her view, Cambodians need at the very least to be able to define what they consider the most and least problematic symptoms in order to redefine PTSD in terms of their own population. However, she questions whether there is even a need to diagnose PTSD when what is required is not to designate people as "sick", but rather to help sufferers see that their responses are perfectly normal under the circumstances and to offer them community-based solutions. There is, of course, another concern about using the concept of PTSD to frame psycho-social distress with reference to children in particular, in that the syndrome was identified in adults and there is little evidence that it has been adequately assessed for validity with children.

Health practitioners in the two systems are sometimes deeply suspicious of each other. In the survey conducted by Brown and Gerber, the *kruu Khmer* were reluctant to refer patients to Western practitioners, preferring to use their own remedies, prayers and water ceremonies. For their part, Western practitioners felt that traditional healers sabotaged "proven" Western scientific methods, such as malaria control. Eisenbruch, though, has not found practitioners in the two systems to be so wary of each other, remarking that some traditional healers, recognizing when they cannot deal with a problem, are happy to refer patients to Western medical practitioners.

Whether or not the two systems can ever coexist more comfortably is in part dependent·on learning more about and working with indigenous categories. Having spent several years studying indigenous diagnoses, taxonomies and treatments with respect to psychological distress and psychiatric disorders in Cambodia, Eisenbruch argues that: "In the Cambodian case, it is difficult to find the indigenous equivalents of the Western illness categories, and a new taxonomy is needed" (1994:23). He has established that, as in Western psychiatry, the *kruu Khmer* use several overlapping taxonomies for mental distress and psychiatric disorder, there being a "cascade from mild dysphoria to frank madness" (1994:4). The taxonomies of the *kruu Khmer* include natural conditions, caused by genetic or constitutional factors, infections, deterioration or accidents, and supernatural conditions which stem from mystical, animistic and magical causes.

The main indigenous category of psycho-social distress or psychiatric disorder is *ckuet*, a condition with multiple causes, manifestations and treatments. Only when a person displays pronounced abnormal behaviour is he or she described as having *ckuet*. Troubled people, on the other hand, are described as "having sorrow and suffering", and this can develop into "damaged heart-mind" when a distressed person becomes disorganized. When someone loses his or her memory, this is regarded as more serious still. Deities are said to induce *ckuet* when they attack people. Ancestral spirits may cause people to have *ckuet* by invading them or removing their protection, often following a lapse in conduct. It is also possible to inherit madness, ancestor madness being the only psychotic condition in the indigenous taxonomy clearly associated with family history.

Eisenbruch cites the illness known as *ckuet sa? te? ?aaram* as being the condition most closely associated with stress, loss and bereavement, social and economic deprivation and family disruption. Such circumstances are believed to lead to "thinking too much", and this has a destructive effect on the human mind. Largely because *ckuet sa? te? ?aaram* is a disorder of thinking, Eisenbruch suggests that it seems to resemble schizophrenia more than any other disorder, although unlike schizophrenia it is not understood to be genetically linked. This is the illness most closely associated with the Pol Pot years, "because the Khmer Rouge used it as an epithet against people who were too 'lazy' and therefore in danger of being executed" (Eisenbruch, 1994:13). Eisenbruch notes that some academics and professionals in Cambodia have an aversion to framing mental disorders within the category *ckuet sa? te? ?aaram* because of this association with Khmer Rouge diagnosis. Some of those who oppose using this framework claim that the illness did not exist before 1975, although the *kruu Khmer* assured Eisenbruch that it is an ancient category. Several traditional healers were cautious about their ability to heal people suffering from *ckuet sa? te? ?aaram*, highlighting the importance of respecting their self-acknowledged limitations with regard to mental health.

As mentioned, the indigenous health system encompasses a range of specialists, from bone setters to the specialist *kruu* who help people in social crises and mental distress, as well as the monks. Commenting on the efficacy of the indigenous system, Drucker notes that:

> Whatever the relative merits of the two cosmologies of medicine, it would be hard to deny how well the ambience created by the traditional healers fits the emotional needs of the Khmer. . . . many of the healers have genuine psycho-therapeutic abilities as well as a strong sense of medical ethics. They are familiar with their neighbours' needs and problems

because they are indeed neighbours, with a common language and culture. . . . (1986:5).

Patients with psychological disturbances — frequently expressed in terms of spirits and "possession" — who might find themselves hurriedly diagnosed by Western medicine as in need of psychiatric help, find that the traditional healers are familiar with such beliefs and well equipped to give appropriate support (1986:4).

It is vital to learn more about the areas in which indigenous models are most effective and this means learning more about indigenous codes and beliefs. On this, anthropologist Adam Kuper notes that "folk models exhibit forms of reasoning which are becoming increasingly familiar in cognitive science" and that there is a need "to penetrate beyond the partial models of the actors and develop a theory about the modes of thought which constitute these exotic worlds" (Kuper, 1992:11). He cites evidence that there are universal ways of classifying nature:

The idea is that folk sociologies may be decoded if their underlying principles of construction are appreciated. They may turn out to have a great deal in common at the level of content — perhaps . . . because they build upon cognitive universals and, in particular, upon universal ways of thinking about nature.

A central theme . . . is the way in which folk models integrate conceptions of social relations and conceptions of nature. . . . folk models . . . bring together human beings and natural objects within a single conceptual space (Kuper, 1992:11).

4.3

Key Policy Debates

Relief or development?

Because of the magnitude of the emergency in Cambodia resulting from both conflict and economic liberalization and mismanagement, the initial focus of aid was on relief, with rehabilitation as a subsequent priority. The first goal was the delivery of essential supplies (mainly food and medicines) and the reconstruction and maintenance of communications, water and sanitation systems and key buildings. Physical reconstruction is vital. Rebuilding lives physically and reinstating the physical symbols of a society in a period of transition from conflict to peace is a public demonstration of confidence in future stability (Gibbs, 1994; Boyden and Goodhand, 1995). Also, the mere presence of international aid workers in the immediate aftermath of conflict can fulfil a vital solidarity or witness function, averting human rights violations and renewed violence. Sometimes the role of outsiders is simply to act as a catalyst in the generation of innovative responses to social problems. In the words of a Cambodian expatriate, "I don't underestimate the problems; we can't solve the problems but we can bring fresh ideas from outside . . . all we can do is bring new ideas".

Once the immediate period of relief and physical reconstruction is over, however, policies and programmes that aim to reinforce family and community resilience and coping in the long term become more relevant and appropriate. Thus, some of the more recent initiatives in Cambodia have focused less on service delivery and more on self-help approaches to poverty alleviation and building capacity locally for sustainable development. In this regard, certain priorities have been identified, including: the empowerment of women and increasing their access to resources generally through credit and small enterprise schemes for especially vulnerable groups, such as female headed households; capacity building of "natural community leaders" in problem-solving and other skills as a means of strengthening civic responsibility and civil institutions; and organizational and human resource development in key government institutions.

The premise underlying the transition from relief to development is that peace has now been established in Cambodia and that it is therefore feasible to build long-term structures and social processes. The perception of Cambodia as a post-conflict society is therefore one favoured by the international community — especially by those who believe the UNTAC operation to have been a success. The reluctance of donors to concede the persistence of very real threats to peace can result in a serious discontinuity between programme strategies and social and political reality:

Last year our [international aid agency] country programme looked much like in any other developing country. It focused on macro-economic development, rural development, employment generation, etc. It basically ignored that this country is still essentially in an emergency situation. . . . Donors are ready to come in with money that they can invest, but it is not money for emergency relief (Head of an international agency).

Community development

Within the framework of a longer term development policy, the interventions of the aid community in the field of psycho-social welfare and social development generally can be divided roughly into two broad approaches: social targeting and community development. Organizations that concentrate their efforts on development at the community level tend to use a predominantly preventive approach, in the sense that by facilitating the reconstruction of community structures and systems they aim to prevent rather than "cure" social, psychological and economic problems. Within this framework, psycho-social interventions are integrated with other community-based initiatives. Children may receive a broad array of services, such as education or health care, but in the main children who might be facing special difficulties — such as those separated from their families — are affected only indirectly by such interventions. On the other hand, organizations involved in socially targeted programmes tend to focus more on remedial interventions. Traditionally in Cambodia provision for children in especially difficult situations, including those suffering from psycho-social distress, falls mainly in this latter category, consisting in the main of special programmes catering for specific vulnerable groups of children.

The community development work of organizations such as Krom Akphiwat Phum and Buddhism for Development is based on the premise that providing support to community structures will ultimately have greater impact in terms of the numbers affected than working directly with the poorest members of society, and will in any case improve the condition of the poorest or weakest members, in addition to being more sustainable and less costly than targeted approaches. Some agencies employing a community development model provide training in welfare and other skills to "natural" community leaders, the underlying premise being that: ". . . in the presence of capable leadership it is often possible for a community to mobilize itself to take care of its poorest members [itself]" (Taylor, 1994:26). The Khmer Buddhist Society, for example, trains natural helpers, community leaders and government officials from all over Cambodia in social work methods. They learn how to assess and deal with social problems at the individual, family and community levels.

Krom Akphiwat Phum holds the ambitious aims of contributing to Cambodia's reintegration by strengthening trust and responsibility in local communities, increasing respect for the dignity of all women, men and children, particularly the poorest and the neediest, and so empowering local people to work together willingly for the good of all. The organization hopes to improve the quality of village life through co-operation, solidarity, self-reliance and interdependence. The programme was initially supported through the capacity building interventions of two volunteers from the Overseas Bureau of Australia (OSB). The aim from the beginning was to help establish a core group of 12 Cambodians trained to manage and maintain an indigenous structure to address development needs at the village level and facilitate local co-operation. The work started by strengthening the leadership and community development skills of the core group so that they could in turn assist village leaders and others in identifying and addressing local needs. The programme brings returnees, internally displaced people and long-term residents together — mixing these groups is considered important for achieving social cohesion. The intention is that communities should develop the capacity to define their needs themselves and take action co-operatively.

It is tempting to think that by encouraging collective action, the empowerment of vulnerable groups and responsible leadership in civic affairs, the social structural problems that are perhaps inherent in Cambodian society, exacerbated by years of conflict, can be addressed directly. But community development models present several problems, especially in the Cambodian context. For one thing, there is the fact, already discussed, that collective action is not an accepted principle:

> Difficulties may . . . arise when cultural concepts of individuality and co-operation are compared with some assumptions inherent in community development philosophy. The autonomy of households within extended families and the division of labour within families, as compared to the group approach within community development, is an example (IPSER, 1993:9).

There is perhaps a fair amount of political ideology and rhetoric attached to many of the community development initiatives in Cambodia, favouring a view of local villages as homogenous, static communities, which masks the complex social reality. There is the question, for example, of how to define "community" in modern Cambodia, given the often arbitrary way this social unit has been constituted — sometimes merely as a result of forced displacement.

> People [agencies] . . . are basing their understanding on an African model developed in the 1970s. We are looking at the wrong models here in Cambodia, both of community and of family. . . . Cultures vary . . . we need to measure the situation now against what it was like before the war. The problem is

that there is very little information on what society was like before the war. But we certainly shouldn't be measuring the Cambodian experience against the model of the noble peasant (Expatriate working in an international aid agency*).*

Some people perceive the village as the "basic building block of Cambodian civil society" (Emerson, 1996:50). But is this really so? The little anthropological evidence available from the years prior to the outbreak of conflict makes this hypothesis seem unlikely. The informal and fluid nature of social organization presents a serious obstacle to development initiatives at this level:

An alternative to state intervention on behalf of the poor is some form of community support. This suggestion is made in spite of the fact that Cambodia does not have a tradition of associations, volunteer groups, trade unions or other networks composed of people who come together for a common purpose. In fact, this possibility appears rather less likely to succeed in Cambodia today than at any time in history: most people have had enough of being cajoled by government officials into participating in collective action for the public good (Taylor, 1994:26).

Ovesen, et al., 1995 contend that, in the absence of any other principle of organization at the village level, the attention paid to the continuous well-being and good-will of the *neak ta* (spirits) possibly constitutes the only focal area of activity in communal life in the village.

There is the additional problem of balancing sometimes acute short-term economic needs and raised expectations with a commitment to the longer term and less concrete aims of self-sustained development:

Building system capacity to implement present and future programmes does not always sit comfortably with the moral imperative to see the delivery of benefits today. Getting people to learn and to take responsibility for their own destiny requires a hands off but supportive approach (Taylor, 1994:24).

People have difficulty thinking about the future. For example, we have set up this fertiliser scheme so that people can have fertiliser on loan, but they are hungry so sell the fertiliser to get food . . . (Khmer woman working in a local NGO).

Agencies working at the community level must opt either to engage with existing community structures or to go beyond these and try to facilitate the formation of new ones that give greater voice to those people who have traditionally been marginalized socially and economically. One advantage of working with traditional structures is that this may provide continuity with the past, thereby helping rebuild social confidence. But reinforcing traditional hierarchies in this way offers no guarantee that the poorest and most vulnerable will benefit. In fact, it may merely serve to entrench pre-existing disparities between the most powerful and those most marginalized. Hence the priority of some agencies to develop new civil institutions and new ways for women and other less powerful groups to gain access to resources and decision-making fora.

Undoubtedly, finding viable institutions and leadership in a society that has long been subject to conflict is a major challenge. That said, religious structures are well developed in many Khmer communities. Indeed, Emerson supports the realization of peoples' "spiritual and practical needs" through "socially engaged Buddhism", noting that: "The *'Sangha'* (the Buddhist body) represents the only remaining 'politically neutral' institution within Khmer society" (1996:50-51). "The potential value of the *Wat* as a community support system and the *Sangha* as a nation-wide network should not be overlooked" (1996:50). Her grounds are that in recent history, most institutions have been compromised by the way they manipulated civilian populations for their own ends: here she is referring specifically to the monarchy, the military and both central and local government. By contrast, the Buddhist *Sangha* was the one institution not implicated in the long years of political violence and, despite the killings of religious leaders in the 1970s, respect for Buddhist monks and nuns and the *Sangha* remains strong. Emerson points to the way in which the *Sangha* combines moral teachings and social welfare, making this institution a particularly suitable one for psycho-social interventions. Several NGOs now work with Buddhist monks from local *wats*. Priority is given to training in community development, social welfare and agriculture so that these religious leaders can provide social support and guidance in their villages: "Once they [the monks] have the knowledge, they will spread the knowledge to the villagers and the children throughout the community" (Local NGO worker).

One major disadvantage of the community development approach in Cambodia, with regard to children specifically, is that it renders them practically invisible, whereas many consider that children in fact play a critical role in the social reconstruction of communities:

> [In] integrated community development work we need to . . . start with the children, as they can teach their parents by example. . . . While the influence of the outside world is one thing that is changing society there was also the Khmer Rouge time, when we learned to kill, we killed animals and humans alike. And this learning is being passed on to children, almost like things are passed from parents to children in their genes. So, we need to socialize children into a new way based on morals and ethics. We teach them about voluntarist values and how many small goods make a big good (Head of a local NGO in Battambang).

As a rule, community development relies on the theory that benefits from aid and from economic development in general will somehow permeate throughout society, even to the "poorest of the poor" and to those most marginal socially, including children who live in exceptionally difficult situations. But this theory was assessed and discredited in several studies in different parts of the world some time ago, since it was consistently found that vested interests at the local level would obstruct the flow of resources to the less powerful; indeed, benefits from community development would sometimes be distributed so unevenly that the more vulnerable members of society would become poorer and more burdened with work rather than less.

Social targeting

Social targeting, in contrast to community development, aims at the very least to provide a safety net for the more vulnerable groups by offering them special services, skills training, credit and other forms of assistance. But some consider that it is not enough to meet the immediate needs of vulnerable groups, since this will not change their status in society or their condition in the long term. Thus, in a more radical version of the model it is seen as having the potential to meet the strategic needs of the poor also. This means removing prejudice and stigma, changing the balance of power, transferring resources to the poor and obtaining equity and social justice for socially marginal groups. These goals are thought to be best met through advocacy, legal aid, legal literacy, capacity-building and other such initiatives. The idea is that rather than facilitate more of the same, social and cultural transformation is necessary as a precursor to real development.

Certainly, directing aid at specific groups in society who are understood to have special problems and special needs has a number of advantages for those concerned with children facing acute social distress. It makes highly specific interventions, psycho-social or others, possible. But targeted approaches also embody a number of problems. Concepts such as "vulnerable group" or "the poorest of the poor" are ill-defined in the context of Cambodia, and may in any case be erroneous given that some 30-40 per cent of the population nationally is struggling to survive. Moreover, as stated already, agency perceptions about vulnerability may be entirely divorced from reality. Indeed, Ovesen et al., note that the groups identified in the development discourse as vulnerable bear no relation to the *neak* categories recognized by Cambodians.

> Development categories are much more situationally political-economic and socio-economic and include (partly overlapping categories, such as) refugees, returnees, poor people, internally displaced people . . . extremely vulnerable individuals . . . and female-headed households. . . . All these are, of course, assumed to be highly relevant categories which it is necessary to identify in order to alleviate the particular problems of the various parts of the population (1995:16-17).

They go on to argue that "development classifications and associated actions sometimes seem to bestow their agents or agencies with an inflated sense of executive power and control over reality" (1995:17). Targeted aid needs understanding of local classifications, effective problem identification and monitoring and must receive long-term support. "Fair and equitable targeting depends on local knowledge and transparent public processes" (Taylor, 1994:20).

Although many agencies are working in creative and positive ways with those they perceive to be the most vulnerable and needy people, one village leader commented that:

> Sometimes international agencies, like the World Food Programme, come here to help but . . . usually the families

that are rich get two rations and the poor families only get one. Even then they sometimes lose it. People are afraid to speak out about this (Phum leader and traditional healer in Battambang Province).

So much was lost even before it arrived at the village. If we are due to receive ten ton of rice it might not be unusual for only half a ton to arrive. Likewise with clothes, we were due to get 10,000 pieces for this area and only 1,000 arrived (Phum leader).

Thus, consciously choosing to work with the most vulnerable can pose serious conceptual, methodological and ethical difficulties:

There is no uniform way to work with vulnerable groups. When we work with one core [vulnerable] group the good thing is that the source of funds is not so complicated, but the bad thing is that when we only work with orphans, for example, there is a danger of socializing them into an orphan world, or with amputees, into a world only of amputees. The words "orphan" and "amputee" and "widow" then become encultured . . . they may feel "we are to be pitied" but we should not pity them, they need compassion and help at integration (Head of a local NGO).

Psycho-social interventions

As far as can be established, it would appear that at one time family and members of villages, such as the village headman, the *kruu Khmer* and the religious leaders, would ensure that the most vulnerable were cared for as best they could. Government was not much involved in mental health or social welfare interventions. During the Khmer Rouge period, such state social services as existed for vulnerable groups were destroyed entirely. Thus, in the absence of community structures and with each individual struggling for his or her own survival, often to the exclusion of all others, the more vulnerable members of the community were by definition in a highly precarious and often fatal situation at this time. During the 1980s, however, socially disadvantaged groups received greater attention when, under the influence of socialist Viet Nam, this kind of welfare intervention became the responsibility of government.

Female-headed households, for example, received some assistance under the *Krom Samaki* system. Similarly, even though funding was a problem, by 1989 some 3,400 children were being cared for in 26 state-run orphanages. The government of the time also operated residential centres for street-people and for the "re-education" of prostitutes.

Mental health and social deprivation are not perceived by many aid agencies anywhere in the world as a priority in emergency relief, but are rather seen as a part of rehabilitation and reconstruction initiatives in the post-conflict phase. Consistent with this international trend, there has been very little programmatic work in Cambodia in the field of mental health particularly, although there have been several social welfare interventions. This gap exists despite the preoccupation with psycho-social issues among aid agency staff and the argument made by observers, such as Emerson and also by NGOs like IPSER, that community development in Cambodia cannot effectively proceed without first addressing the massive psycho-social damage due to decades of conflict. "In a country where as many people have been mentally scarred by violence as Cambodia, attention to psycho-social problems is a necessary condition for successful community development" (IPSER, 1993:5).

In terms of the current availability of services for vulnerable groups, the situation is poor because the government is struggling to keep up even with "mainstream" issues. The Ministry of Social Affairs (MSALVA) and the Ministry of Women's Affairs have limited human and financial resources. Many of their policies are in the early stages of development and it will take time for them to become fully operational. However, the government runs 26 orphanages for children in 15 provinces, a significant proportion of the children in these centres having physical or mental disabilities (de Monchy, 1991). Attempts are being made to find alternatives to the institutionalization of vulnerable groups. A sub-committee on street people for the municipality of Phnom Penh has been set up, for example, to try and assist people to return to their home provinces (UNICEF, 1995). While during the 1980s the services for people with disabilities focused in the main on the provision of prosthetics, new initiatives have been instigated in which the government is co-operating with NGOs to address their more complex social problems.

But the efforts of central government in this field remain very limited and the present shortage of public sector resources has in the main left multilateral and non-governmental agencies in charge of providing for the most vulnerable members of society. Many of the agencies that engage in community development at the village level would no doubt maintain that these initiatives have impacts, even if indirect, on the psycho-social well-being of especially vulnerable groups. UNHCR, Help Age International, Redd Barna, CWDA and several others, however, all direct their programmes exclusively at specific vulnerable categories or groups. UNHCR's "safety net" programme, for example, is designed to support female headed and other households whose income is revealed, by a home assessment, to be exceptionally low. The provision includes credit, although the tendency is for people to consume this because of overall scarcity of resources.

Even with these initiatives, provision for the most vulnerable groups by international and local NGOs remains scant and poorly developed, especially when set against the large amount of foreign aid disbursed in Cambodia. Such work is still comparatively new to the country, and in some cases, the problems are simply too great to allow for easy solution. The sexual exploitation of women and children and domestic violence, for example, are widespread and entrenched phenomena that, in the absence of an effective and functioning judicial system, are extremely difficult to tackle. Likewise, although there are a number of agencies (CMAC, MAG, The HALO Trust and COFRAS) working on de-mining and mines awareness, mines "are being used for activities such as fishing, guarding one's property, settling disputes, as well as, in some situations of domestic violence" (UNICEF, 1995). The dangers caused by mines will therefore persist until their use becomes socially unacceptable. Moreover, mines continue to be laid by both the government and the Khmer Rouge and both have refused to give permission for de-mining in certain areas — despite the number of civilian casualties (Expatriate worker at the Mines Advisory Group; Uimonen personal communication).

Many agencies approach psycho-social issues not so much from a "mental health" perspective as from one framed by and integrated with the theory and practice of social welfare or social work. This applies to many of those organizations, such as Krom Akphiwat Phum, Cambodia Family Development Services (CFDS) and Khmer Buddhist Society, supporting community development for example. Others have mounted more specialized social welfare schemes. Save the Children Fund UK, for instance, is providing a team of people to work with MSALVA on the development of social policy and practice and establishment of mechanisms for aid co-ordination. Although there are some interesting and potentially very important initiatives in this area, there is a general disquiet among aid agency staff that social work interventions run by people trained as social workers — whether professionally qualified or para-professionals — cannot deal adequately with individual mental distress or psychiatric disorders. It is the feeling that there is more to do specifically in mental health that drives much of the discussion in expatriate circles about psycho-social issues, collective psychosis or mass trauma and PTSD.

Specific emphasis is given to mental health and psychiatric issues in a few outpatient programmes, there being no inpatient facilities in Cambodia (Winkelmann 1996:48). Adults receive consultations in Phnom Penh and Siem Reap hospitals, and there is a service for children in Kandal hospital. Winkelmann has undertaken a survey of clinical facilities for mental health and psychiatric disorders in Cambodia. Drawing on personal communications with K. Sunbaunat of the Ministry of Health Mental Health Sub-Committee in Phnom Penh in 1996, she states that among adult patients, 25 to 30 per cent are diagnosed with "depression" and another 25 to 30 per cent with "anxiety" and "post-traumatic personality changes", the remaining having "psychotic" conditions or alcohol-related problems. She also notes that in 1995 the hospital in Kandal province registered 126 patients under 18 years of age, of whom half were diagnosed with "mental retardation", "schizophrenia" or "behaviour disorders". The outpatient department in Kandal is supported by Caritas and the Dr. Marcel Cahrle Roy Foundation and receives referrals from Medicine de l'Espoir (Winkelmann, 1996:72).

The Harvard Programme in Refugee Trauma Cambodia (HPTC) in Siem Reap, following research conducted by Dr. Richard Mollica and colleagues in the Thai border camps, operates entirely within a Western biomedical framework and is soon to initiate a training programme for 50 doctors annually. Out-patient psychiatric evaluations and clinical treatments are provided, in the provincial hospital, together with follow-up and counselling services, which are complemented by community-level training of teachers and soldiers in the identification of psychoses and referral systems. Although operating in a framework more directed at Khmer conceptions and values, IPSER probably also veers more towards mental health than social welfare interventions. However, the agency collaborates closely with organizations such as the Khmer Buddhist Society (KBS), which employ social work models, and has a strong programme of outreach in which the aim is to support local structures and institutions, including traditional healers. IPSER focuses on Battambang province and Odong district near Phnom Penh and is involved in collaborative training relationships with KBS and the Cambodia Mental Health Training Programme (CMHTP). The CMHTP, funded by the International Organization for Migration (IOM), from Norway and the Ministry of Health, is a three year psychiatric training programme for 10 Cambodian doctors who are based at the Preah Norodom Sihanouk Hospital.

While there is a concern that mental health should be given greater priority in Cambodia, it is often recognized by the foreign community that to respond to psycho-social distress with narrowly-defined mental health interventions following the biomedical model, using experts in diagnosis and treatment and caring for patients individually, often in secondary health facilities, would not be appropriate:

> . . . you can't take a trauma programme alone because there are other issues. That's why we don't do such programmes (even though it is one of our main interests). People here are actually so wrapped up with on-going poverty, hunger and domestic violence; it's not their main problem. . . . The problem with sending people to hospital is that it is just overloaded and some of the people we are sending probably don't really need to go. Even if they do go and are able to be seen there are sometimes problems with the availability of an appropriate drug (Expatriate aid worker).

It is also questioned whether such a model can be sustained in a poor country like Cambodia.

Sometimes we don't have enough money for the drugs . . . At the moment we get our drugs from a British agency. There are only three organizations in the whole of Cambodia that have access to this medication . . . . Sometimes when I do have the drugs I can't do the analysis of the blood count to find out if the medication is having any effect. . . . Doctors working here want to have a mental health hospital, but it wouldn't be sustainable, it would just become a prison for people. We had one hospital like this but it was really terrible. People are used to being in a community and it is not the answer to put them into a hospital (Expatriate Cambodian aid worker).

Some expatriates, acknowledging that the Western and Cambodian health systems can be complementary, have sought to develop therapeutic models that harness the skills and beliefs of both. Dr. Heigel, for example, persuaded some of the Western doctors in the Thai camps to work with the *kruu Khmer* in a cross-cultural collaboration. Likewise, IPSER maintains that a primary health and community development programme cannot promise to treat the whole spectrum of psycho-social, psychosomatic and major psychiatric disorders in a community and must therefore work with the monks and *kruu Khmer*. The agency provides training in practical and theoretical psycho-social skills to community workers (teachers, healers, health and welfare workers) so that they can help the most vulnerable groups to cope with their traumatic experiences and take control of their fate and lives. The goal is to prevent serious long-term medical, psychological and psychiatric consequences of conflict by using a public health approach in combination with psycho-social intervention strategies.

Because of their social standing, the *kruu Khmer* can mobilize others to deal with a host of medical, social and domestic problems. Of course, the low cost of traditional therapies is another advantage. "Under the care of the *kruu* many symptoms of depression disappear without prescribing scarce and expensive drugs" (Drucker, 1986:6).

Traditional treatments consist of the manipulation of limbs, application of ointments, blowing on patients, rubbing the back and top of the head, astrological readings, recitation of mantras and the provision of herbal remedies. Meditation and relaxation relieves anxiety symptoms. Prescribing traditional botanical or pharmaceutical remedies can help those with psychosomatic or autonomic symptoms. Some healers have the ability to exorcise spirits, helping those who believe they have been invaded by a malevolent spirit (IPSER, 1993:6). Eisenbruch has identified more than 100 monks and *kruu Khmer* in every province in Cambodia, and his database, in addition to giving special areas of clinical interest or expertise, training, diagnostic systems and methods of treatment used, includes information concerning the expressed willingness of traditional healers to collaborate with health and community development work.

Whatever the potential of working specifically on mental health issues, whether with indigenous healers or not, it is striking that in the work carried out to date children receive very little attention specifically. There seems to be a tacit assumption that adults are a greater priority in this respect, possibly because the victims of Cambodia's greatest catastrophe, the violence of the Pol Pot years, are now all adults. Or it could be because the status of children's mental health is thought to derive largely from that of their parents or other prime carers and it follows, therefore, that to assist the adult is, automatically, to help the child. This is an assumption that fits neatly with the research conducted in Europe after the Second World War, but it is also one that cannot be made without proper substantiation in the Cambodian context. Evidence from other conflicts certainly suggests that psycho-social distress can be transmitted through the generations and so it is important to consider the consequences for children even when they have not been exposed directly. However, the link between the parental condition and that of the child is but one factor to be taken into account and cannot be taken as a reliable predictor of children's psycho-social well-being.

Interaction between Cambodian and external aid models

In so far as the aid community is now a major player in Cambodia, it can make a major contribution to the resilience of children and their families. But aid also has the capacity to increase vulnerability, creating dependency or inciting conflict and corruption, particularly in resource-scarce societies (Boyden and Goodhand, 1995.; Gibbs, 1994). Sometimes the changes associated with aid interventions bring no tangible benefit. As an elderly man in Phum Somnagn said: "interventions from outside do change things . . . they move things from one difficulty to another difficulty".

Whatever the effect of aid disbursements, the sector certainly provides employment. This point has been made by a monk working for a local NGO, who remarked that Cambodians have learned to adapt to the "land-cruiser culture" of the aid community as the best means of getting a job. And another man, working for an international agency, frankly admitted:

> I'm glad the international organizations are here: they help the middle class . . . to find work. What would I do without the NGOs? I suppose I could work for the government, but I would have to be involved in corruption to survive. Or I could be a commander in the army, but again I would have to tell the soldiers to make money for me so that I could survive. Yes, I'm glad the international organizations are here.

It is sometimes impossible to contain problems that are the unanticipated effect of intervention. This was certainly the case with the UNBRO border operation, which facilitated the rehabilitation of Khmer Rouge remnants and restored their fighting capacity. Frequently, aid impact is undermined by poor communication between aid agencies and aid recipients.

We feel that it must be difficult for the international community to understand us. One day we are looking out, hoping so much for the rain. But when it comes, it comes too much. Its difficult to explain this to foreigners. First we ask for food because of flooding, then we ask when it's too dry!
(Phum leader).

Aid is often "packaged and delivered" in forms that do not coincide well with actual conditions and needs at the grassroots level. Sometimes, it is delivered with strings attached, forcing communities and families to develop ingenious strategies to ensure that they qualify (Boyden, 1994). Strategies such as these may enhance family coping, while at the same time they increase the vulnerability of children. For example, family size has been used as a criterion affecting the amount of money awarded by UNHCR to Cambodian returnees. This encouraged many families to take in unaccompanied children and claim them as their own so as to increase the rations. These children were subsequently abandoned during the return to Cambodia and some are now confined to local orphanages where conditions are extremely poor. Many other returnee families split up, individual members going to different parts of the country, so as to increase access to UNHCR's "family package". The intention may have been to rejoin one another once back in Cambodia, but often this has not proved possible, with the result that a significant number of families remained separated.

The way in which children themselves actively and often very skilfully take advantage of the rules and regulations of aid interventions is well illustrated by the following example.

A Khmer woman's childhood experiences:
A disabled mother, on hearing of the imminent take-over by the Khmer Rouge and knowing that it was unlikely that she would be able to take care of her daughter (about 5 or 6 years old at the time) sent her to Thailand to stay with relatives. The girl ended up in the north with her grandmother, where she stayed some time. However, as it was not possible for her to be educated there, she later travelled south to stay with her uncle, who was working in the military in the refugee camps on the border.

She found she was unable to stay with her uncle in the military barracks and had to register herself as an unaccompanied minor so as to receive free food, clothing and education. In order to do so she had to say that she had been separated from her family. Having listened to some of the other children talking about their situations, she decided that she would pretend to be the missing sister of one of the unaccompanied boys. She built up a picture of this boy's life, then constructed hers to fit it. Although at first he denied that she was his sister when the authorities asked them their stories separately they were remarkably similar and in the end she managed to persuade both the officials and the boy himself that she was indeed his sister.

When the time for resettlement arrived, they were resettled together in the United States. But all the time she had to continue living the lie — even sitting through ceremonies for "their" dead parents while silently hoping that her real parents were in fact alive.

As a teenager in the States she told this story in confidence to one of the refugee workers with whom she had become friendly. When this person, now working in Cambodia, last heard from her, she had still not told her "brother" and was concerned that he might discover the truth when he returned to Cambodia in 1995, the first time since the repatriation.

It is vital to draw on local knowledge and concerns as a basis for programme and policy planning and development. Yet identifying the needs of the Khmer people as understood and articulated by them, rather than delivering pre-packaged programmes, implies the use of participatory methods that are as yet little known or utilized in Cambodia:

> I think what people should do is go into villages and find out exactly what people need. It is for the people to design and determine what they really need, not the agencies (Local NGO worker in Battambang).

> A more flexible — community based — approach is possible, if organizationally expensive. This involves working with the people to get them to identify their priority needs and problems and then to devise ways of solving them, with the outside agency working in the role of facilitator rather than executor (Taylor, 1994:23).

Sometimes development thinking is in direct contradiction with the Cambodian world view. This point is made powerfully in an appraisal of Swedish official aid policy by Ovesen et al. They cite the ways in which this policy runs counter to existing social processes and trends in Cambodia:

> While the political system since Angkorian times has been highly centralized, one aim of Swedish efforts is a decentralization of the administration.

> While social relations in all sectors of society have been ruled by a strict and pervasive hierarchy, development should entail democracy and relative equality.

The attainment of equality is deemed especially important in the sphere of gender relations, where traditional Khmer culture has favoured the ideological subordination of women.

Development is per definition a process of change that will make the future significantly different from the past, whereas the 'conservatism' of Khmer culture takes its model of the perfect society from a (mythologized) social order in the past.

While development stresses the ability of people to determine and change their own future situation through concrete actions, Buddhism teaches that destiny is a result of the individual's *karma* and that a person's positive actions create merits which will only be beneficial in future incarnations (1995:16).

Certainly some aid agencies have very ambitious plans for social change in Cambodia, to bring the country as far as possible into line with the Western model of democracy. So it is that democracy, good governance, civil society and civil and political rights have all come to dominate the aid agenda in recent years partly as a result of the continued security problems, corruption and human rights violations. This has drawn some agencies away from their traditional field of so-cial and economic development. There now function in Cambodia some highly specialized NGOs whose work bears little relation to conventional NGO activity. The Mines Advisory Group, for example, exists exclusively to respond to the safety problems posed by the mines. Others (such as Licadho, Adhoc and The Coalition for Peace and Reconciliation) are involved in monitoring, lobbying and campaigning on civil and human rights issues. There is great potential for this kind of work to contribute both to economic and political stabilization and to the achievement of local "ownership" of governance and human rights issues. While those who have lived in Cambodia for many years have born witness to a significant expansion in civil society organizations, there are others in the international community who are impatient and, perhaps, have unrealistic expectations of the pace of change.

Many things are worse now than before [1970]. We should look at what responsibility the West has in this. The people working here are sincere but people always look to their own politics, whatever fits their own policies. It is very sad: they speak of these beautiful concepts, but they are just empty words. After fifteen years of strict socialism [we are forcing] them straight into democracy and human rights and freedom, not because it is good for them, but because it is good for our governments (International aid worker).

The government has, in a way, proved a reluctant partner in the transition to a democratic society. It may be aware that economic development is necessary to stop the return of the Khmer Rouge, but still asserts political control to a degree that undermines development (International aid worker). Suppression is seen as the best way of crushing any opposition, even though this policy is highly risky given that the benefits of the recent economic boom are so poorly distributed.

Unfortunately, the government does not have a sense of urgency about delivering economic development, the only long-term strategy being to direct people not to have any aspirations. The doctrine of control and power is the only doctrine. Government refers to "Angkor" society as the ideal, which was a slave society anyway (International aid agency worker).

4.4

Institutional Trends

Aid as a political instrument

Many see aid interventions in Cambodia as presenting serious institutional or funding shortcomings. Referring to the very difficult years immediately after the downfall of the Khmer Rouge, Commander Sir Robert Jackson (Under-Secretary General and Senior Advisor to the United Nations) argued that:

. . . whenever considering the Kampuchean tragedy, it is essential always to keep in mind two fundamental facts. First, rarely in history has the entire population of a nation been subjected to such bestial and inhuman treatment as that endured by the Kampuchean people under Pol Pot. . . . Second, in my experience, no humanitarian operation in this century has been so totally and continuously influenced by political factors . . . (Mysliwiec, 1988:iii).

That there exists today much debate and some self-doubt within the aid community in Cambodia as to its impact and role is hardly surprising given the changes of aid policy over the last few decades. The distortion of aid distributions by political considerations has at times seriously undermined political and social reconstruction. Thus, a policy of strident aid conditionality, predicated largely on political and human rights grounds, has oscillated with one in which serious problems of governance are ignored and large sums of money made available with scant regard for their utility or effect. While conditionality in itself presents many problems, flooding a country with funds when the absorptive capacity is very limited has a debilitating effect on government and society as a whole.

Aid policy proved to be no more consistent after the withdrawal of the Vietnamese troops and the opening up of the Cambodian economy in 1989. The international community conceded to the Khmer Rouge joining the peace talks, for example, failing to comment on their appalling human rights record. And even today, although many people express concern about suppression and control by government, most agencies hold back open criticism for fear of political destabilization. Serious corruption among senior public officials remains a grave problem, largely ignored by the international community.

There is a lot of unconditional money coming into Cambodia from bilateral donors. . . . This is a face-saving exercise. Because of the 2 billion dollars invested in the peace process, the international community can't afford to admit it's a mistake. The community wants peace at any price (International aid agency employee).

Half the government's budget is given by the IMF and the World Bank but the international community doesn't put on any pressure. The government is still giving over half their budget to the military. And there is so much corruption (Expatriate aid worker).

Thus, while donors talk about the need for democracy and peace, in the face of continuing human rights abuses and infringements on the freedom of organization and speech, around half of central government expenditure still goes to defence. Some question whether multilaterals such as the IMF and the Word Bank, who make very significant contributions to the public sector budget, should not ensure that less of that money is spent on defence. However, the fact that many aid contributions are an integral part of trade agreements affects this policy. As European Union Ambassador Gwyn Morgan explained:

The reason why we are in Cambodia is to encourage stability and democracy in this area, which is a major area of interest for Europe. . . . Co-operation to Cambodia is based on certain principles, which the government understands and we understand (**Phnom Penh Post**, 8-21 September 1995).

An international NGO worker commented: "Sometimes donors argue that they feel bound to support the military endeavour in order to meet security concerns". She noted that one bilateral donor recently gave $3 million to a military counter-insurgency school, the justification being that: "money allocated for community development projects and hospitals could not be used effectively unless security was assured, which made their support for the military essential".

Problems of co-ordination

Lack of co-ordination among aid agencies in Cambodia is another factor identified as a problem by several aid personnel in multilateral agencies, international NGOs and local NGOs, largely because of its destabilizing effect. McAndrew puts many of the aid co-ordination problems down to competition between agencies for a space in which to operate.

> As aid flows increased to Cambodia, competition arose as new organizations sought to establish their respective niches. Once it became clear that donors held different views on how the development process should unfold, on how priorities should be set, and on how sector programmes should be designed, co-ordination broke down. Conflicts also surfaced as agencies manoeuvred for project contracts, for control over sector work, for staff in local institutions, and for donor country resources (1996:15).

Poor co-ordination has adverse impacts at the local level:

> In certain communes you can find more than one NGO working there — in most cases you see that they are not working together. But co-ordination is so important, not just between NGOs but also between NGOs and the government (Cambodian NGO worker).

Disagreement between the European Union and a number of mainly international NGOs is one of the more extreme examples of recent problems of co-ordination within the aid community. The European Union has been criticized for the way in which it disburses aid in Cambodia. Before the elections the EU was investing heavily in Battambang and Pursat provinces, but it has now withdrawn from the area, redirecting support to six provinces around Phnom Penh. An

NGO worker in Battambang noted that "The European Union stayed here two years, then pulled out. They cut the aid very suddenly . . . it was not very elegant" (Quenelle, 1995:8). NGO workers question the motives for this hasty move: was the initial involvement merely aimed at securing the elections and facilitating a subsequent transfer closer to Phnom Penh, where the EU would be more visible and its operations more convenient? Many NGOs also fear that with US $ 87 million to spend on rehabilitation in only 30 months, the EU "may duplicate, and even threaten existing (NGO) projects. . . . Thirty months is not enough. It [the PERC scheme] will collapse, with bad impacts for the NGOs' work afterwards" (Quenelle, 1995:8).

Some argue that the problem of co-ordination is often due to personality clashes between agency personnel, as well as a sense of territoriality: "Local NGOs can't see the light in each other's eyes. They are very competitive and aggressive towards each other" (International aid agency worker). There is often direct competition over funds:

> There are so many problems between agencies here: agencies accusing each other of plagiarism — and they are so competitive, lacking any ability to collaborate and to share information (International consultant).

Some agency personnel attach a measure of responsibility for poor co-ordination to government:

> Part of the problem of co-ordinating the aid coming into the country is that there are often misunderstandings [within government] about how to deal with donors. For instance, they may ask a number of different donors for the same thing and then when the donors get together and realize that they are all being asked to give money for the same thing, they say no (Head of an international aid agency).

Importantly, there have been a number of efforts recently to improve aid co-ordination, at both the policy and institutional levels. "Co-ordination is a major problem here, but we have started to make real efforts in this field" (Head of an international aid agency). Although the government still has no official NGO co-ordinating body, the NGOs have set up two umbrella groups (the NGO Forum and the Cambodian Co-ordination Committee) of their own. These bodies, to which member NGOs contribute fees, deal with both substantive issues of policy and practice and co-ordination, organizing workshops, commissioning research, and similar activities. Collaboration between international and local NGOs has led to the formation of several issue-focused working groups. One such group is concerned with monitoring the Convention on the Rights of the Child and another centres on the sexual exploitation and trafficking of children.

Government has been brought together with local and international NGOs on several occasions to attend thematic workshops. In 1995, for example, the Ministry of Social Affairs hosted a workshop in Battambang on children's issues, with contributions from local government and a variety of NGOs with a local presence. And part of the function of the Save the Children Fund (UK) technical experts in the Ministry of Social Affairs is to improve co-ordination between government and the aid sector.

Lack of absorptive capacity

The total amount of external multilateral and bilateral assistance pledged to Cambodia between 1992 and 1995 amounted to US $2,288 million. Of this, only 58.9 per cent (US $1,346 million) was in fact disbursed (CDC/UNDP Development Cooperation Report 1995 cited in McAndrew, 1996:3). McAndrew questions whether such large amounts of aid can be effectively managed in the short term or whether it would not be better to give smaller amounts but spread over a longer period. Certainly this might be the case. However, "donor programme cycles are short term and appropriations often subject to annual approval". He goes on to note that "particularly in times of crisis aid flows are not necessarily adjusted to the needs and absorptive capacity of the recipient country, but more attuned to the political needs of donors seeking to manifest foreign policy" (McAndrew, 1996:4).

The lack of absorptive capacity within government specifically has been cited as an important reason for its inability to respond to the demands of a large-scale aid commitment. It is the view of some expatriates that aid agencies take insufficient account of what Cambodians have been through in recent decades and fail to understand the difficulties of coping with the onslaught of aid activity:

> People in government have said to me that they are simply overloaded and that the international community is expecting too much from them. They say 'we are operating on a fifth grade level, but the donors expect us all to operate at graduate level' (International aid agency worker).

> . . . I find that some people in government are ready to give up because the international community is pushing them too hard. It is not surprising, then, that when we make a suggestion they say: 'yes, that's good, please will you do it'. It is also true to say that often people here accept advice as an order (Head of international aid agency).

> Several times I have been told by the Khmer to take it slowly. . . . It is crazy for us to think that we can bring in these ideas and that they will just be accepted. . . . There are all these concepts coming in, but attempts to make these concepts their own are lacking (International NGO worker).

One expatriate aid worker observed that government officials, for their part, fail to acknowledge the value of external assistance, taking into account only those funds passing directly through line ministries and ignoring the operational programmes of international agencies that are being executed alongside public sector interventions — work in fact done on behalf of government. In her opinion public sector officials lack an understanding of what the proper and appropriate relationship between government and other civil society actors should be, although she did concede that this is hardly surprising given Cambodia's political isolation in recent decades.

To gain the skills necessary to develop more constructive relations with the aid community, the government requires assistance with both human resource and institutional development. In the absence of such initiatives, donors will no doubt continue to express little faith in the public sector, preferring instead to support NGOs and grassroots organizations. This of course raises a set of very different issues connected with outreach and sustainability.

Changing roles of NGOs

Because of the crisis of governance and the consequent economic decline bedevilling Cambodia in recent years, non-governmental organizations have been forced to work in ways that are new and challenging. The work on psycho-social issues, for example, is a radical departure from tradition for many. But there have also been some important institutional developments. In some functions they have replaced government, while in others they have worked alongside it. By force of circumstance, many have had to work on a scale beyond their traditional scope:

In 1979 the Kampuchean tragedy opened a new chapter in NGO history. It challenged their traditional roles, causing them to reflect and redefine their philosophies and approaches to development work. Most NGOs found themselves struggling with internal conflicts in the contrast between this role and their more traditional types of activities. Not only were they dealing with aid on a far larger scale than usual, they were handling projects whose size defied their traditional 'small scale, grassroots, self-help' mandate. Additionally, they found themselves working with and through government institutions rather than local organizations and with a socialist government unacceptable to and unrecognized by virtually all Western governments (Mysliwiec, 1988:68).

Much of the original aid intervention in Cambodia in the post-Democratic Kampuchea phase was managed by international NGOs who were directly operational. The first Cambodian NGOs emerged out of local human rights initiatives in support of the elections during the UNTAC period (de Monchy, 1994). In line with efforts internationally to support self-sufficient and sustainable development, there has been a marked trend to "indigenize" the NGO sector in the last few years. This trend is supported by several parallel processes, as one local NGO worker explained:

Firstly, there are those local NGOs that have set up on their own, they have their own goals and interests. Secondly, there are those local NGOs that start to work with an international partner from the beginning, but who have a clear goal that the NGO will become wholly Cambodian in some time. Thirdly, there are those 'unexpected local NGOs'. These come into being on the back of a contract from an international NGO, and fourthly, there are those that are set up by the Khmer team when the international NGO staff they had been working with leave (Cambodian community development worker).

The number of local NGOs involved in development work is increasing. In Battambang, for example, there were only 7 in 1992 but today there are around 40 (ODA, 1993). The number of International Agencies in the area has, however, remained relatively constant, at around 30.

Even though the process of "indigenization" is as yet incomplete, in that international NGOs still employ a large number of expatriate workers and policies and programmes are very much determined by their foreign founders and/or funders, the speed of this process is a major concern to many, expatriates and Cambodians alike.

> Although we talked altogether [Khmer and expatriate staff] about how much longer the programme needs foreigners here and came up with a date in 1996 for the expatriates to withdraw, the Cambodians keep saying that they are not ready for us to go yet. . . . It's really very difficult to decide at what point we should leave (International NGO worker in Battambang).

In Battambang the pressure on international NGOs to indigenize is mounting in the face of the imminent termination of block grant funding in several cases and calls from head offices to withdraw international staff. But what are the motives for such developments? Is indigenization sustainable? And how is it being achieved?

One advantage of indigenization may be the replacement of external understandings of and responses to psycho-social distress with indigenous approaches. However, in many ways the agendas have been set even before the process has been completed: NGO policies draw on pre-existing models employed in other conflicts; strategies for intervention are already largely set within the frames of biomedicine or social work; the classifications of vulnerability are defined by outsiders and staff training is also conducted by outsiders. There is a need to let the Khmer set their own agendas, use their own expertise in psycho-social issues, and only import external ideas and approaches where the indigenous model is lacking.

Some are suspicious that international NGOs are building the capacity of their Khmer staff simply to facilitate a withdrawal of foreign funds from Cambodia, as has occurred in other societies in transition. Of course, the need for capacity building in Cambodia is acute given the long years of isolation, but there should be continued financial support until indigenous initiatives can become self-sufficient. In the absence of sufficient managerial and professional skills within Cambodia, some observers point to the potential for expatriate Khmer to assume senior roles in NGOs, but this raises other problems:

> Many expatriate Cambodians come back and feel that they ought to have all the top positions, but they are often inappropriately equipped and the Cambodians that have stayed feel that the Cambodian expatriates are disrespectful of them (International agency worker).

Obviously, one reason why there is a human resource problem in the sector is precisely the reliance on imported policies and programmes, which require a high level of expertise and minimal grassroots para-professional involvement: "The problem with people buying into the Western models is that it only leads to professionalization and then the consequent brain drain" (International consultant). One international development worker questioned the validity of training people to a professional level in Cambodia — since this will most likely be a waste of resources, given that people of high status are unlikely to be prepared to take up a post in the backwaters of Cambodia where the need for skilled personnel is greatest.

Conclusions and Recommendations

The impact of political violence on children, their families and communities is a major international concern, not just to those affected but also to governments, national and international aid agencies and welfare workers. The key question for many is how best to respond, how best to help affected communities cope with adversity.

Cambodia is emerging from one of the most devastating conflicts of this century. In so far as international aid agencies are now disbursing significant sums of money in Cambodia to support the reconstruction process, they are in a position to make an important contribution to the coping and resilience of individuals, families and communities at the local and national levels. For the international community to respond appropriately, however, requires not only an understanding of how the specific cultural context influences the way in which the psycho-social impacts of political violence are experienced by people but also of how the wider socio-economic, historical and political environment gives rise to various constraints and opportunities.

In the immediate aftermath of the most intense period of violence, the initial focus of aid was on relief, with rehabilitation as a subsequent priority, although the majority of agencies have now made the transition to a more developmental approach. Thus, recent initiatives include building the capacity for sustainable development through credit and small enterprise schemes for vulnerable groups, training "natural" community leaders in problem-solving and other skills and providing technical assistance on organizational and human resource development to key government institutions. Aid has also been used to facilitate the rebuilding of essential services such as health and education, which are vital to recreating a state of normalcy for Cambodian children. And as a result of continued security problems, corruption and human rights violations, subjects such as democracy, good governance and civil society have also come to dominate the aid agenda.

Nevertheless, aid has a patchy history in Cambodia having been manipulated at times by powerful political interests outside the country. Important work to uphold the peace process and reinstate essential services and infrastructure, for example, has been undermined by decisions at the international level which give greater weight to geopolitical considerations than to humanitarian need. In resource-scarce societies, poorly designed and implemented interventions can increase vulnerability by creating dependency or inciting corruption, problems that are prevalent in Cambodia. Other concerns include the excessive demands of aid practitioners on debilitated government structures, lack of co-ordination or friction between aid agencies and top-down approaches to programming.

Careful monitoring and evaluation of the impact of aid in Cambodia is urgently needed, especially with regard to psycho-social interventions: how effective, for example, are the various approaches in Cambodia in responding to people's distress? And what about aid strategies such as the indigenization of non-governmental agencies? The feasibility of such approaches under present conditions and circumstances in Cambodia needs careful assessment, as does the strong reliance on community development models imported from other parts of the world. Spreading awareness about the role of aid, including constraints and limitations, is also important. Better advocacy and closer collaboration between the various aid agencies and other civil society actors would lay a stronger foundation for programmatic work. Mechanisms for aid co-ordination should be strengthened, so that the policies of different agencies are more consistent. Greater emphasis needs to be given to institutional and human resource development at the national and local levels within both the governmental and non-governmental sectors. Attention should be paid not just to the coverage of services but also to their content. In education, for example, curriculum, teacher training and delivery mechanisms merit attention if the system is to contribute to the maintenance of peaceful values and cater to the needs of a modern democratic state.

Western ideologies have had a profound influence on aid policy and interventions in emergencies and inform the discourse as to who is most affected and in what ways they become vulnerable. The Western therapeutic model in particular attributes psycho-social distress to the individual and devises responses based on drug therapy or the talking out of personal difficulties. But this approach presents some serious problems. It is, for example, in direct opposition to models founded on a holistic cosmological system, such as that which exists in Cambodia, in which aggrieved ancestors, malevolent spirits and other forces play a crucial part in both the cause and cure of psycho-social distress. Moreover, individual therapy conducted by a medical expert can undermine the spontaneous efforts of families and communities to provide support and care. The relevance, appropriateness and feasibility of employing theoretical models based on Western biomedical notions of health and illness in societies that have very different ontologies and social and cultural forms is increasingly being brought into question. Aid practitioners and theorists are now doubting the validity of Western psychiatric models across cultures, for even though the physiological experience of distress may have certain universal characteristics, the ways in which people express, embody and give meaning to that distress is largely dependent on context. Close consideration of the possible drawbacks of employing this kind of therapeutic model in Cambodia is needed prior to intervention.

Western thinking also involves strong views about childhood, seeing it as a time of vulnerability and dependence, and children are often viewed as the passive victims of conflict. Accordingly, children are believed to be especially and universally susceptible to political violence, the recipients of experience rather than the active negotiators of it. Yet, evidence from research in a number of countries suggests that the impact of violence on children is quite unpredictable. Many children show remarkable resilience in the face of extreme stress. This has led some people to search for those factors which mediate impact. Children have access to a broad range of resources — personal, social, economic and cultural — which even in the most extreme circumstances can provide protection against psycho-social distress. By the same token, the absence, destruction or distortion of such resources can greatly increase their susceptibility. A lot more needs to be learned about children's coping strategies, resilience and vulnerabilities, as well as the structural factors that mediate the impact of political violence on their lives. Information of this nature could be of great value in developing culturally sensitive, sustainable interventions that facilitate and build on the creative ways in which people are reconstructing their lives, both as individuals and as members of broader social alliances.

More than two decades of political violence in Cambodia have had a devastating effect on health and survival, family life, civil society, and the national economy, making social reconstruction, forgiveness and healing seem remote and implausible. Cambodia does not yet enjoy political stability, democracy or peace and remains prone to the vola- tile forces of economic liberalization and rapid social change. Family separation, displacement, death, landlessness and destitution are problems affecting many Cambodian children today. The adverse psycho-social impacts of long-term exposure to violence and social disruption are frequently mentioned by both expatriates and Cambodians. Concern is expressed, for example, about the prevalence of values, attitudes and practices learned during the years of conflict which are believed to be counter-cultural or dysfunctional. The greatest preoccupation is with trafficking in children, criminal and domestic violence and other forms of abuse.

That there are a large number of vulnerable people in Cambodia today is also understood to be a direct consequence of armed conflict. The aid community has identified several categories of people it believes to be the most socially and economically marginal, the most prone to exploitation and abuse. Included among these categories are street children, orphans, young combatants and those exploited sexually. But these categories do not necessarily fit Cambodian classifications of vulnerability. Psycho-social distress among Cambodians manifests itself through the prevalence of fear, distrust, guilt and shame and lack of hope and self-esteem. And somatic symptoms, depression and other psychological phenomena are also said to be extremely common. Most of the information on psycho-social distress in Cambodia is anecdotal, however, there being very little systematic evidence, especially with regard to children.

Given the shortage of reliable information, the inconsistencies in the therapeutic models employed in Cambodia and the complexity and pervasiveness of the violence of recent decades, finding a conceptual framework for interpreting and responding to psycho-social distress is an extremely difficult task. As the head of one UN agency commented:

> We just have no theoretical model to deal with a situation as complex as the one here in Cambodia. We simply don't know how to do it. At a meeting attended by the heads of the UN

agencies in Turin earlier this year we discussed this in depth. We looked at governance, social regeneration and the alleviation of poverty. But with psycho-social issues — and how to support social regeneration — we got stuck. We couldn't find a way to go forward.

Learning about the psycho-social impacts on children in particular is more challenging still, largely because issues to do with children or childhood are subsumed under discourses about the disintegration of the family, the problems of female-headed households or domestic violence. The only attempts to research the psycho-social condition of Cambodian children have been among refugees, using Western theory and Western diagnostic instruments.

There are few programmes in Cambodia geared specifically to mental health, although a large number provide for social welfare through community development work or initiatives directed at especially vulnerable groups. Most of these interventions are led by expatriates and based on universal assumptions and universal therapeutic models drawn from the biomedical and social work traditions. Employing notions of individual pathology and using Post Traumatic Stress Disorder to explain pathological conditions is entirely unfamiliar to the majority of Cambodians and may be of little relevance to their coping or healing. Some expatriates, arguing that the Western and Cambodian health systems can and should be complementary, have sought to develop therapeutic approaches that harness the skills and beliefs of both. Traditional healers and auxiliary health workers have played a vital part in some of this work. More should be done to encourage and disseminate such initiatives.

The focus on individual functioning and individual pathology in Western mental health responses detracts from the broader structural consequences of conflict. Political violence has many adverse impacts on children and adults that are social or economic rather than mental.

Effective programmes and policies in the psycho-social field need to be inclusive and multi-sectoral, to address social as well as mental health issues. An integrated approach such as this would fit more closely with the holistic Khmer cosmology. Besides, working with individuals is not sustainable in a country like Cambodia, where so many people have been affected by violence and where the very fabric of society has been undermined. Borrowing from the field of physical health, low-cost preventive psycho-social measures at the grassroots level should take precedence over secondary care in specialized institutions using specialized technologies.

Because understanding and meaning play such a vital part in the processing of grief and psycho-social healing generally, it is important to draw as much as possible on local constructions and interpretations of conflict as well as local therapeutic approaches and strategies. A baseline assessment is also required to provide a more accurate picture of the incidence of psycho-social distress, the forms it takes and its distribution within and across various sectors of society. As a part of this exercise, the coping mechanisms of individuals, families or households, communities and other groups should be documented so that the aid community can reinforce or build on existing mechanisms and strategies.

External models should be used only in those cases where indigenous strategies offer no solution. A concerted effort is needed to learn more about Cambodians' perceptions of pathology in mental health and social behaviour so as to render more effective and appropriate the psycho-social interventions of the international community. Experience from other post-conflict societies would suggest that psycho-social healing and social reconstruction cannot be managed by outsiders. Greater effort needs to be given to collaborating with the *kruu Khmer*, monks, nuns and others in Cambodia who traditionally assist individuals and families to resolve their problems. Aid agencies can do much to reinforce the moral authority and leadership of these people and to help them become more effective in their work.

Healing and reconstruction can best be facilitated by a balance of preventive interventions at the local level and more targeted remedial programmes supporting the most disadvantaged sectors of society. Work within villages, however, must take into account concepts of collective organization and responsibility that are meaningful to the people themselves rather than building on ideals about rural community life that come from other parts of the globe. It is also worth remembering that constant exposure to social engineering and political violence in recent history has left a poor legacy in Cambodia for communalism or collective action. On the other hand, breaking away from community development approaches and targeting the poorest of the poor or the most disadvantaged socially presents problems of sustainability and stereotyping and makes little sense in the long run without more radical and strategic efforts to meet the needs of those who are vulnerable.

Support for further research on psycho-social issues is an area in which international agencies can play an effective part. As already stated, information is required on Cambodian children specifically, as well as on the social structural, cultural, economic and political factors that influence the attempts of families and individuals to rebuild their lives. At a practical level, though, learning about the nature and extent of people's distressing experiences and the degree to which these have had an impact on their lives presents a serious problem in a country like Cambodia where so many have been affected. There is also the added difficulty of developing methods for gathering information that are appropriate to the cultural and social context and to the issues in question. Most psycho-therapeutic models in the West are based on the assumption that talking about and sharing a sense of grief or loss is an essential part of healing. But grief may be a very private process supported more effectively by spiritual belief than external intervention.

In Cambodia, people who have undergone profoundly stressful events are not necessarily able to talk about them, whether for cultural or other reasons. Developing research methods for investigating sensitive and potentially distressing issues with children and adults is a major consideration in itself, especially if children's views are to be listened to with respect and children are not to be rendered more vulnerable by the research process. Methods beginning with structured questionnaires and checklists have no real place in research on psycho-social issues with children.

There are a number of alternative approaches to research, which are more participatory, and more respectful of children's right to privacy and their right not to be hurt by intrusive questioning. In this kind of approach children are treated not merely as informants or research subjects, but as social agents with an active part to play in decisions affecting their lives. In Cambodia, children have participated very little, if at all, in the debates about psycho-social distress or trauma or for that matter the role of aid. It is worth noting that Cambodian children may well have quite a lot to say on these issues, and that they are very likely to know quite a bit about their condition and their needs. They might also be able to contribute important ideas about the measures most effective for ameliorating or ending their psycho-social distress. This may seem a rather novel approach, but it is one being employed to great effect in other countries with other groups of children, such as street and factory workers. Thus, a carefully planned process of consultation and research *with* Cambodian children, rather than investigations *of* Cambodian children, could provide the most sound basis for future planning in the psycho-social field.

Bibliography

Allen, T. (1989)
"Violence and moral knowledge: Observing social trauma in Sudan and Uganda", **Cambridge Anthropology**, Vol.13 No. 2, pp. 45-66.

Baker, A. (1990)
"The psychological impact of the Intifada on Palestinian children in the occupied West Bank and Gaza: An exploratory study", **American Journal of Orthopsychiatry**, Vol. 60, No. 4, October, pp. 496-505.

Ben-Ezer, G. (1990)
"Anorexia Nervosa or an Ethiopian coping style? Diagnostics and treatment of an eating disorder among Ethiopian immigrant Jews", **Mind and Human Interaction**, Vol. 2, No. 2, pp. 36-39.

Bernander, B., Charny, J., Eastmond, M., Lindahl, C. and Öjendal, J. (1995)
Facing a Complex Emergency: An Evaluation of Swedish Support to Emergency Aid to Cambodia, Sida, Stockholm, March.

Bit, S. (1991)
The Warrior Heritage, a Psychological Perspective of Cambodian Trauma, Seanglim Bit, El Cerrito, California.

Boothby, N., Upton, P. and Sultan, A. (1991)
Children of Mozambique: The Cost of Survival, US Committee for Refugees, Issue Paper, Washington D.C., November.

Boyden, J. (1994)
"Children's experience of conflict related emergencies: Some implications for relief and policy and practice", **Disasters**, Vol. 18, No. 3, September, pp. 255-267.

Boyden, J. and Goodhand, J. (1995)
   NGO Capacity-Building in North West Somalia: A Concept Paper, INTRAC (The International Training and Research Centre), Oxford, November.
Bracken, B.J., Giller, J.E. and Summerfield, D. (1995)
   "Psychological responses to war and atrocities: The limitations of current concepts", **Social Science & Medicine**, Vol. 40, No. 8, pp. 1073-1082.
Bromley, M.N. (1987)
   "New beginnings for Cambodian refugees — Or further disruptions?", **National Association of Social Workers Inc.**, May-June, pp. 236-239.
Brown, S. and Gerber, L. (1992)
   Development of an Integrated Healing Model to Address the Mental Health Crisis among Khmers, mimeo, World Rehabilitation Fund Inc. and the University of New Hampshire International Exchange of Experts and Information in Rehabilitation, Washington D.C.
Burman, E. (1994)
   Deconstructing Developmental Psychology, Routledge, London.
Cairns, E. (1987)
   Caught in Crossfire, Children and the Northern Ireland Conflict, Appletree, Syracuse University Press, Belfast.
_____ (1996)
   Children and Political Violence, Blackwell Publishers Ltd., Oxford.
Dafar, M.A. (1988)
   "An analytic review of the general causes of psychological problems among Afghan refugee children", in Psychiatry Center for Afghan Refugees, **The Impaired Mind**, Peshawar.
Davenport, P., Healy, J. and Malone, K. (1995)
   Vulnerable in the Village: A Study of Returnees in Battambang Province, Cambodia, with a Focus on Strategies for the Landless, OSB/WV Australia.
Dawes, A. (1992)
   Psychological Discourse about Political Violence and its Effects on Children, paper prepared for the meeting: The Mental Health of Refugee Children Exposed to Violent Environments, Refugee Studies Programme, University of Oxford.
Dawes, A. and Tredoux, C. (1989)
   The Impact of Political Violence on Children: A Study from South Africa, paper presented at The Fourth Ethnography of Childhood Workshop, Victoria Falls, Zimbabwe.

de Monchy M. (1991)
Children in Especially Difficult Circumstances, consultancy report,
UNICEF-Cambodia, Cambodia, June-September.
_____ (1994)
Cambodia Case Study, for the Conference on the Rights of the Child,
The Hague, 20-21 June.
de Waal, A. (1989)
Famine that Kills: Darfur, Sudan, 1984-1985, Clarendon Press,
Oxford.
Drucker, D. (1986)
"Human oneness: Traditional healing in a refugee situation, **UNICEF
News,** New York.
Duffield, M. (1994)
"Complex political emergencies and the crisis of developmentalism",
IDS Bulletin: Linking Relief and Development, Vol. 25,
No. 3, October.
Duffy, T. (1994)
"Towards a culture of human rights in Cambodia", **Human Rights
Quarterly,** Vol. 16, pp. 82-104.
Ebihara, M. (1968)
Svay, a Khmer Village in Cambodia, Columbia University Ph.D.,
United States.
Ebihara, M. (1993)
Beyond Suffering: the Recent History of a Cambodian Village,
Harvard Institute for Development, USA.
Eisenbruch, M. (1991a)
"From post-traumatic stress disorder to cultural bereavement: Diagnosis
of Southeast Asian refugees", **Social Science and Medicine,**
Vol. 33, No. 6, pp. 673-680.
_____ (1991b)
**Traditional Healers as Harbingers of Cambodian Culture:
Cultural Survival as a Social Responsibility for International
Mental Health,** background paper for congress plenary session on
21 August, 1991 World Congress, World Federation for Mental Health,
Mexico, 18-23 August.
_____ (1994)
**Resources and Limitations in Meeting The Health Needs of the
Cambodian Population,** paper presented at the conference: Mental
Health Education for Medical Doctors in Cambodia, Phnom Penh,
19-21 April.

Emerson, B. (1996)
**A Legacy of Conflict; Trauma as an Obstacle to Poverty
Alleviation in Rural Cambodia. A focus on Women,
Empowerment, and NGO Initiatives,** Masters of Social Science
in Rural Development Dissertation, Development Administration Group,
University of Birmingam, March.

Foong, L.H. (1995)
**Cultural Contexts of the Readjustment Process among Amputees
in Cambodia; Future Research Directions,** mimeo, Johns Hopkins
University, Baltimore, 11 January.

Freeman, M.D.A. (1993)
The Rights and Wrongs of Children, Frances Pinter Publishers,
London.

Gabarino, J. (1991)
Children in Danger: Coping with Community Violence, paper
presented at the meeting on Mental Health Issues of Refugee Children
Exposed to Violent Environments, Refugee Studies Programme,
University of Oxford.

Gabarino, J., Kostelny, K. and Dubrow, N. (1991)
No Place to be a Child, Lexington Books, New York.

Geertz, C. (1973)
The Interpretation of Cultures: Selected Essays, Basic Books Inc.,
New York.

Gibbs, S. (1994)
"Post-war social reconstruction in Mozambique: Re-framing children's
experience of trauma and healing", **Disasters,** Vol. 18, No. 3,
September, pp. 268-276.

Gibson, K (1989)
"Children in political violence", **Social Science and Medicine,**
Vol. 28, No. 7, p. 659-668.

Gilmore, D. (1990)
Manhood in the Making: Cultural Concepts of Masculinity,
Yale University Press, New Haven.

Goodhand, J. (1994)
**Dancing with the Prince; The Role of Indigenous NGOs in
Complex Political Emergencies with Reference to Afghanistan,**
M.Sc. Dissertation for degree course, "Community organisations for
rural development", University of Manchester.

Gorden, D. (1988)
"Tenacious Assumptions in Western Medicine", in Lock, M. and
Gorden, D. (eds.), **Biomedicine Examined,** Kluwer Academic

Publishers, Dordrecht, pp.19-56.
Greer, J. (1985)
"Viewing 'the other side' in Northern Ireland: Openness and attitudes
to religion among Catholic and Protestant adolescents", **Journal for the
Scientific Study of Religion**, 24, 3, pp. 275-92.
Harmer, A. (1995)
**Rebuilding War-Torn Societies: Psycho-Social Vulnerability and
Coping Mechanisms in Cambodia: A Feasibility Study**, mimeo,
Phnom Penh.
Hay, L. and other students from Vocational Training Centre for Disabled (1993)
A letter from a Khmer Amputee, translation by Ouk Rathanak,
edited by Josephine Barbour, Battambang, Cambodia.
Human Rights Vigilance of Cambodia (1995)
**Combating Women Trafficking and Child Prostitution: Results
from Rapid Appraisal on Child Prostitution and Trafficking**,
mimeo, Cambodia.
Ingham, J. (1996)
Psychological Anthropology Reconsidered, publication of the
Society for Psychological Anthropology, No. 8, Cambridge
University Press.
IPSER (1993)
**Psycho-Social for Cambodia: A Programme to Support
Individuals, Families and Communities in Overcoming Trauma**,
Institute for Psycho-Social and Socio-Ecological Research, Maastrict.
IRC Oral History Project (1990)
**Displaced Lives: Stories of Life and Culture from the Khmer in
Site II, Thailand**, International Rescue Committee, Bangkok.
Jackson, T. (1987)
**Just Waiting to Die — Cambodian Refugees in Thailand:
Report of a Tour to the Thai-Cambodian Border and
Subsequent Research**, mimeo, Oxfam, Oxford, July.
Jama, M. (1992)
The Girl Child in the Situation of Emergency: Case of Somalia,
paper presented at UNICEF regional workshop, Gaborone, Botswana,
6-8 July.
Jennar, R. (1991)
**The Cambodian Gamble: Three Months of Negotiations Towards
a Peace Fraught with Dangers**, NGO Forum on Cambodia,
Phnom Penh.

211

_____ (1992)
Cambodia between UNAMIC and UNTAC, NGO Forum on
Cambodia, Phnom Penh.
_____ (1992/1994)
Cambodian Chronicles: Numbers 2-12, NGO Forum on
Cambodia, Phnom Penh.
Kinzie, J.D., Sack, W.H., Angell, R.H., Manson, S. and Rath, B. (1986)
"The psychiatric effects of massive trauma on Cambodian children, I:
The children", **Journal of the American Academy of Child
Psychiatry**, Vol. 25, No. 3, pp. 70-79.
Kuper, A. (1992)
"Introduction" to Kuper, A. (ed.), **Conceptualizing Society**,
European Association of Social Anthropologists, Routledge,
London.
Ledgerwood, J. (1992)
Analysis of the Situation of Women in Cambodia, Phnom Penh.
Ledgerwood, J., Ebihara, M and Mortland, C. (1994)
"Introduction", in Ebihara, Mortland and Ledgerwood (eds.),
Cambodian Culture Since 1975: Homeland and Exile,
Cornell University Press, Ithaca.
Leyens, J. and Mahjoub, A. (undated)
The Psycho-Social Effect of War on Children and Adolescents,
mimeo of the Catholic University of Louvain-la-Neuve, Belgium.
Lock, M. and Schepher Hughes, N. (1990)
"A Critical-interpretative approach in medicinal anthropology:
Rituals and routines of discipline and dissent", in Johnson, T. and
Sargent, C. (eds.), **Medical Anthropology: Contemporary Theory
and Method**, Praeger, New York, London.
Marston, J. (1994)
"Metaphors of the Khmer Rouge", in Ebihara, Mortland and
Ledgerwood (eds.) **Cambodian Culture Since 1975: Homeland
and Exile**, Cornell University Press, USA.
McAndrew, J. (1996)
**Aid Infusions, Aid Illusions: Bilateral and Multilateral
Emergency and Development Assistance in Cambodia,
1992-1995**, Cambodia Development Resource Institute,
Phnom Penh, January.
McCallin, M. and Fozzard, S. (1991)
**The Impact of Traumatic Events on the Psychological
Well-being of Mozambican refugee Women and Children**,
International Catholic Child Bureau (ICCB), Geneva.

McCallin, M. (1991)
   **The Psycho-Social Consequences of Violent Displacement:
   The Experience of Central American Refugee Women in
   Washington DC,** International Catholic Child Bureau (ICCB), Geneva.
Meas, N. with Healy, J. (1995)
   Towards Restoring Life: Cambodian Villages, JSRC, Phnom Penh.
Metraux, C. (undated)
   **Training Techniques of Non-Professionals in a Framework of a
   Preventive and Primary Care Programme in Mental Health,**
   mimeo, Centre d'étude de la famille, Clinique Psychiatrique
   Universitaire de Cery, Switzerland.
Miligram, R. and Miligram N. (1976)
   "The effect of the Yom Kippur War on anxiety level in Israeli children",
   Journal of Psychology, Vol. 94, pp.1063-1075.
Mollica, R. et al. (undated)
   **Repatriation and Disability: A Community Study of Health,
   Mental Health and Social Functioning of the Khmer Residents
   of Site II,** mimeo, Harvard Program in Refugee Trauma, Harvard
   School of Public Health and the World Federation for Public Health:
   **Volume 1: Khmer Adults: Working Documents; Volume II:
   Khmer Children (12-13 years of age).**
Mysliwiec, E. (1988)
   Punishing The Poor: The International Isolation of Kampuchea,
   Oxfam, Oxford.
ODA (1993)
   **Survey of NGO Activity in Battambang Province — Cambodia,
   1993,** ODA Battambang Urban Water Development, Survey carried
   out September-November.
Ovesen, J. Trankell, I. And Öjendal, J. (1995)
   **When every Household is an Island: Social Organization and
   Power Structures in Rural Cambodia,** preliminary draft report
   commissioned by Sida, Stockholm, November.
Parker, M. (1995)
   War and The Mind, paper presented at the 9th Bio-social Meeting,
   Oxford, 5 May.
Punamaki, R.L. (1987)
   **Children under Conflict: The Attitudes and Emotional Life of
   Israeli and Palestinian Children,** Tampere Peace Research Institute
   Research Reports, No. 32, Tampere, Finland.

Punamaki, R. (1989)
"Factors affecting the mental health of Palestinian children exposed to political violence", **International Journal of Mental Health**, 18, 2, pp. 63-79.

Quenelle, B. (1995)
"Funding giant faces its critics", **Phnom Penh Post**, 8-21 September, p. 8.

Ressler, E., Boothby, N. and Steinbock, D. (1988)
Unaccompanied Children: Care and Protection in Wars, Natural Disasters and Refugee Movements, Oxford University Press, Oxford.

Ressler, E., Tortorici, J.M. and Marcelino, A. (1992)
Children in Situations of Armed Conflict: A Guide To The Provision of Services, UNICEF, New York.

Richman, N. (1992)
Annotation: Children in Situations of Political Violence, mimeo, draft report, London, September.

Richman, N. , Ratilal, A. and Aly, A. (1989)
The Psychological Effects of War on Mozambican Children, mimeo, Ministry of Education, Mozambique.

Roberts, S. and Williams, J. (1995)
After the Guns Fall Silent: The Enduring Legacy of Landmines, Vietnam Veterans of America Foundation, Washington, D.C.

Rutter, J. (1994)
Refugee Children in the Classroom, Trentham Books, London, UK.

Scheper-Hughes, N. and Lock, M. (1989)
"The mindful body: A prolegomenon to future work in medical anthropology", **Medical Anthropology Quarterly**, Vol. 3, No. 1, pp. 6-41.

Schildkrout, E. (1978)
"Roles of children in urban Kano", in La Fontaine, J.S. (ed.), **Sex and Age as Principles of Social Differentiation**, Academic Press, London.

Summerfield, D. (1991)
"Psychological effects of conflict in the Third World", **Development in Practice**, Vol. 1, No. 3, pp. 159-173.

Summerill, K. (undated)
Appropriate Mental Health Service for Cambodian Refugees, mimeo, Berkeley, California.

Taylor, A. (1994)
Poverty in Cambodia, a Review carried out for UNICEF-Cambodia as part of its Country Situational Analysis, Phnom Penh.

Thion, S. (1993)
     Watching Cambodia, White Lotus, Bangkok.
Tickner, V. (1996)
     Food Security in Cambodia: A Preliminary Assessment", UNRISD
     Discussion Paper No. 80, UNRISD, Geneva, October.
Turton, R., Straker, G. and Moosa, F. (1991)
     "The experiences of violence in the lives of township youth in 'unrest' and
     'normal' conditions", **South African Journal of Psychology**, Vol. 21,
     No. 2, pp. 77-84.
Uimonen, P. (1994)
     **Responses to Revolutionary Change: A Study of Social Memory
     in a Khmer Village**, Masters thesis, Stockholm University, Department
     of Social Anthropology, October.
UNDP (1994)
     The Human Development Report, Oxford.
UNICEF (1990)
     Cambodia: The Situation of Children and Women, Phnom Penh.
     _____ (1995)
     Situation Analysis of Children and Women in Cambodia, draft
     report, Phnom Penh, 15 September.
UNRISD (undated)
     **Research Proposal: Vulnerability and Coping Strategies in
     Cambodia**, Geneva.
     _____ (1993)
     Rebuilding Wartorn Societies, report of the workshops on The
     Challenge of Rebuilding Wartorn Societies and The Social
     Consequences of the Peace Process in Cambodia, Geneva, 27-30 April.
Utting, P. (ed.) (1994)
     **Between Hope and Insecurity: The Social Consequences of the
     Cambodian Peace Process**, UNRISD, Geneva.
Vail, P. (1993)
     Savage Semantics, unpublished memorandum.
Vanistendael, S. (1995)
     **Growth in the Muddle of Life, Resilience: Building on
     People's Strengths**, ICCB, Geneva.
Williams, D. (1996)
     Modernising People: NGOs in the Development Process, paper
     presented at a workshop on NGOs at St. Peter's College,
     Oxford, January.

Williamson, J. and Moser, A. (1987)
Unaccompanied Children in Emergencies: A Fieldguide for
Their Care and Protection, International Social Service, Geneva.

Winkelmann, A. (1996)
A Study of Mental Health Approaches in Response to the
Psycho-social Problems Experienced by Repatriated Refugees
in Cambodia, M.Sc., International Health, Queen Margaret College,
Edinburgh, 30 August.

Woodhead, M. (1990)
"Psychology and the cultural construction of children's needs",
in James, A. and Prout, A. (eds.), Constructing and Reconstructing
Childhood: Contemporary Issues in the Sociological Study of
Childhood, Falmer Press, London.

_____ (1996)
In Search of the Rainbow: Pathways to Quality in Large Scale
Programmes for Young Disadvantaged Children, Bernard Van Leer
Foundation, The Hague, The Netherlands.

Working Group on Aid Co-ordination (1995)
The Struggle for Rice, Fish and Water: Cambodians Efforts to
Break Common Ground in Pursuit of Alternatives, Phnom Penh.

Young, A. (1982)
"The anthropologies of illness and sickness", in The Annual Review
of Anthropology, 11, pp. 257-285.

Young, A. (1990)
"Discourse on stress and the reproduction of conventional knowledge",
Social Science and Medicine, Vol. 14B, pp. 133-146.

Zimmerman, C. (1994)
Plates in a Basket Will Rattle: Domestic Violence in Cambodia,
The Asia Foundation, Phnom Penh.

Zwi, A., Macrae, J. and Ugalde, A. (1992)
"Children and war", The Kangaroo, pp. 46-57, year 1, No. 1,
December.

Printed in Switzerland.
GE.97-01537–June 1997–1,000

UNRISD/REPORT/97/2